THE THIRD WAVE

An Entrepreneur's Vision of the Future

STEVE CASE

SIMON & SCHUSTER PAPERBACKS

New York London Toronto Sydney New Delhi

Simon & Schuster Paperbacks
An Imprint of Simon & Schuster, Inc.
1230 Avenue of the Americas
New York, NY 10020

First Simon & Schuster paperback export edition April 2016

SIMON & SCHUSTER PAPERBACKS and colophon are
registered trademarks of Simon & Schuster, Inc.

Chart on page xvii by Kodiak Starr. Graph on
page 168 courtesy of the Kauffman Foundation.

For information about special discounts for bulk purchases, please
contact Simon & Schuster Special Sales at
1-866-506-1949 or business@simonandschuster.com.

The Simon & Schuster Speakers Bureau can bring authors to your live
event. For more information, or to book an event, contact the Simon
& Schuster Speakers Bureau at 1-866-248-3049 or
visit our website at www.simonspeakers.com.

Book design by Ellen R. Sasahara

Manufactured in the United States of America

3 5 7 9 10 8 6 4 2

ISBN 978-1-5011-4075-4
ISBN 978-1-5011-3260-5 (ebook)

*To the entrepreneurs who inspire me
by striving to change the world*

Climb high,
Climb far,
Your goal the sky,
Your aim the star.

—MARK HOPKINS

CONTENTS

FOREWORD *by Walter Isaacson*   xi

PREFACE   1

ONE   *A Winding Path*   9

TWO   *Getting America Online*   27

THREE   *The Third Wave*   42

FOUR   *Start Up, Speed Up*   56

FIVE   *The Three P's*   68

SIX   *Pardon the Disruption*   80

SEVEN   *The Rise of the Rest*   89

EIGHT   *Impact Investing*   106

NINE   *A Matter of Trust*   114

TEN   *The Visible Hand*   145

ELEVEN   *America Disrupted*   165

TWELVE   *Ride the Wave*   185

ACKNOWLEDGMENTS   201

NOTES   207

INDEX   211

FOREWORD

BY WALTER ISAACSON

I HAPPENED TO be a bystander at one of the most important moments in the turn-of-the-century transition to digital media, and the setting could not have been more incongruous. We were at the Great Hall of the People in Beijing for the celebration of the fiftieth anniversary of the Communist revolution in China when this milestone of capitalism occurred.

As part of a 1999 "news tour" organized by *Time* magazine, of which I was editor, we brought the Time Warner board and other American business leaders to China. The capstone was attending a twelve-course banquet for a thousand people at the Great Hall, hosted by the country's top Communist leaders.

My main memory was watching Ted Turner, then vice chairman of Time Warner, glide among the gilded red velvet chairs as he introduced people to "my commie pinko wife," Jane Fonda. But out of the corner of my eye, I kept noticing

Steve Case, with his placid face but intense eyes, in earnest conversation with Time Warner CEO Jerry Levin and board members such as Merv Adelson.

There was a lot of huddling going on, and it intensified just after the dinner. An epic rainstorm erupted, trapping us on the portico and steps of the Great Hall as we waited for our cars. Turner and Case engaged in the bantering they both did so well. Your big conglomerate, Case taunted, can't seem to get us home. "Your billions aren't getting you anywhere, either," Turner replied.

But this was more than banter. Their comments hinted at a deeper truth. That night, with Chairman Mao beaming down from hundreds of huge posters, Case and the Time Warner leaders began discussing how the sprawling old media company, which made movies and magazines and cable television, and the hot online service, which had made "You've got mail" a national pastime but was now threatened by the web and the emergence of broadband, might want to join forces.

Jerry was affecting the air of a wise pasha, listening and nodding. Steve was feigning a casual and laconic aura, as if the possibility of a merger was a topic of only mild curiosity to him. It was clear to me—or perhaps became clear to me in retrospect—that something serious was going down. The following January, less than four months after that evening when the idea was first broached, the merger of AOL and Time Warner was announced.

I had first met Steve in 1992, when AOL and *Time* magazine

became partners in offering online content. His company had just gone public with a $70 million valuation. By the merger eight years later, AOL was valued at $160 billion.

Steve had many great insights back when AOL was a startup, all of them explained in this book. From the day it launched its first service in 1985, when just 3 percent of Americans were online, Steve believed the digital realm was not going to just be about content and commerce. First and foremost, he insisted, it was going to be about fostering community—about connecting people and allowing them to communicate. When I was working on a profile of Steve for my book *The Innovators: How a Group of Hackers, Geniuses, and Geeks Created the Digital Revolution*, Steve told me: "Our big bet, even back in 1985, was what we called community. We thought the killer app of the Internet was going to be people."

Steve was right. AOL tapped into the desire to communicate, connect, collaborate, and form community. The advent of social networks, from Facebook to Twitter to Snapchat to Reddit, has built on that trend. But in many ways, those new services are just a return to the central insight that Steve had when building AOL.

A related insight that Steve had, and which helped create the digital revolution, was the importance of being inclusive. Before AOL came along, the Internet had been a workspace and playground for hard-core geeks, not for ordinary folks who would thrill at a voice saying, "You've got mail." Case and AOL helped lead that change, truly getting America online.

The previous year, then-senator Al Gore—in an act that should have inoculated him from the unfair jokes about having "invented" (a word he never used) the Internet—had sponsored and helped pass a bill that opened up the Internet to commercial and public use. Until then, it had been a network restricted primarily to researchers and government contractors. His bill said that the Internet should be accessible even to those who got online through AOL or other consumer services. "It now seems really silly, but up until 1992, it was illegal to connect a commercial service like AOL to the Internet," Case recalls.

This transformation began when AOL opened a portal in September 1993 to allow its members access to the newsgroups and bulletin boards of the Internet. The deluge was called, especially by contemptuous veteran netizens, "the eternal September." The name referred to the fact that every September a new wave of freshmen would enter college and, from their campus networks, get access to the Internet. Their postings tended to be annoying at first, but within weeks most had acquired enough netiquette to assimilate into the Internet culture. The floodgates that AOL opened in 1993, however, produced a never-ending flow of newbies, overwhelming the social norms and clubbiness of the Net. Many Internet old-timers complained. But, in fact, the democratization of the Internet by AOL and similar service providers was an amazing and wondrous moment. It opened the way for our inclusive and explosive digital revolution.

In this book, Steve Case has recounted these and other lessons from his career and interwoven them with a forward-looking guide on how to succeed in the next wave of innovation. Having helped create the First Wave of the Internet, and then been an active investor in the Second Wave, Steve is uniquely able provide a framework for envisioning how the Internet will be fully integrated into every aspect of our lives.

The Third Wave is a delightful read, and by writing it Steve has performed a valuable service. As someone who has spent more than two decades watching Steve, learning from him, and marveling at his insights, I am thrilled that this book will allow countless future innovators to do the same.

Walter Isaacson, the CEO of the Aspen Institute, is the author of *The Innovators: How a Group of Hackers, Geniuses, and Geeks Created the Digital Revolution* and of biographies of Steve Jobs, Albert Einstein, Benjamin Franklin, and Henry Kissinger.

THE THREE WAVES OF THE INTERNET

FIRST WAVE
1985 → ≈1999

BUILDING THE INTERNET
Laying the foundation for
the online world

DRIVEN BY

PEOPLE

PRODUCTS

PLATFORMS

PARTNERSHIPS

POLICY

PERSEVERANCE

SECOND WAVE
2000 → ≈2015

**APP ECONOMY AND MOBILE
REVOLUTION**
Search, social, and
ecommerce startups grow
on top of the Internet

DRIVEN BY

PEOPLE

PRODUCTS

PLATFORMS

amazon · waze

Snapchat · facebook

Google

THIRD WAVE
2016 →

INTERNET OF EVERYTHING
Ubiquitous connectivity
allows entrepreneurs
to transform major,
real-world sectors

DRIVEN BY

PEOPLE

PRODUCTS

PLATFORMS

PARTNERSHIPS

POLICY

PERSEVERANCE

?

PREFACE

I SPENT A fair amount of my senior year in college hiding away in the stacks of the library, reading and rereading a new book I couldn't put down. It was *The Third Wave*, by futurist Alvin Toffler, and it completely transformed the way I thought about the world—and what I imagined for its future.

Toffler wrote about a coming global transformation. In his telling, the "First Wave" of humanity was the settled agricultural society that was dominant for thousands of years. The "Second Wave" was the post–Industrial Revolution world, where mass production and distribution transformed how people lived. Toffler's "Third Wave" was the information age: an electronic global village, where people could access an endless array of services and information, participate in an interactive world, and build a community based not on geography but on common interests. He predicted the world as we know it today. His vision captivated me. I knew I wanted to be part of that Third Wave. Indeed, I wanted to be part of making it happen.

Preface

In the more than thirty years since the birth of America Online, the Third Wave that Toffler predicted has indeed come to pass. I was lucky to have been there at the beginning, and luckier still to have been a part of it ever since.

The Internet age has progressed at a remarkable pace since those early days. It has had several phases of evolution, too—its very own Toffleresque waves.

The First Wave of the Internet was all about building the infrastructure and foundation for an online world. These were the companies—Cisco Systems, Sprint, HP, Sun Microsystems, Microsoft, Apple, IBM, AOL—that were working on the hardware, software, and networks that would make it possible to connect people to the Internet, and to one another. Together, we were building the on-ramps to the information superhighway. (Remember that term?)

Back then, our band of online pioneers had to fight for everything. We had to fight to reduce the cost of getting connected, as telephone networks were typically charging $10 per hour to get online, making it unaffordable for most. We had to beg PC manufacturers to consider shipping their computers with built-in modems. At the time, only hobbyists were online, and most PC executives couldn't fathom why any normal person would ever need a modem.

In the early days of AOL, so much of our job was just explaining what the Internet was, how it worked, and why anyone would want to use it. I remember doing an interview in 1995 on PBS where I was asked, "Why do people need this?" This question was still an open one at the time. And that was a *decade* after we got started.

Getting people online gave the next generation of innovators a new canvas and new paint. Great minds started considering the vast applications of global connectivity. They tinkered and fiddled, then chased ideas and started companies. (One of our users got his start in coding by hacking AIM, or AOL Instant Messenger, communications software. His name was Mark Zuckerberg.)

The Second Wave of the Internet began at the turn of the twenty-first century, just in time to inflate the dot-com bubble and let it burst—the Internet's first real extinction event. A lot of entrepreneurs and investors lost fortunes. But those who survived were primed to lead the next era of Internet innovation.

The Second Wave was about building on top of the Internet. Search engines like Google made it easier to explore the sheer volume of information available on the web. Amazon and eBay turned their corner of the Internet into a one-stop shop. It was during the Second Wave that social networking came of age, too. Where Google sought to organize the Internet's information, social networks let us organize ourselves—and attracted a billion users. And it was during the Second Wave that Apple introduced the iPhone, Google introduced Android, and a mobile movement was born. This convergence supercharged the Second Wave, as smartphones and tablets became the engines of the new Internet, creating an economy that would populate the world with millions of mobile applications.

The Second Wave has been largely defined by software as a service—social apps like Twitter and Instagram that make sharing ideas and photos easier, or traffic apps like Waze, which weren't practical without ubiquitous mobile connectivity. And while the most successful of these companies all dealt with unique obstacles to climb to the pole position, they also have a great deal in common. First, their products are, practically speaking, infinitely scalable. Coping with new users is usually as simple as adding more server capacity and hiring more engineers. And, second, the products themselves—the apps—tend to be infinitely replicable. Nothing has to be manufactured.

Today, the Second Wave is starting to give way to something new. Decades from now, when historians write the story of technological evolution, they will argue that the moment the Internet became a ubiquitous force in the world was when we started integrating it into everything we did. This moment is the beginning of the Third Wave.

The Third Wave is the era when the Internet stops belonging to Internet companies. It is the era in which products will require the Internet, even if the Internet doesn't define them. It is the era when the term "Internet-enabled" will start to sound as ludicrous as the term "electricity-enabled," as if either were notable differentiators. It is the era when the concept of the Internet of Things—of adding connected sensors to products—will be viewed as too limiting, because we'll realize that what's emerging is the much broader Internet of Everything.

The entrepreneurs of this era are going to challenge the biggest industries in the world, and those that most affect our daily lives. They will reimagine our healthcare system and retool our education system. They will create products and services that make our food safer and our commute to work easier.

But if this new generation of entrepreneurs is to succeed, the playbook from the Second Wave won't do.

Third Wave company creation stories are less likely to begin with dorm-inspired apps that go viral, as they often did in the Second Wave. Third Wave entrepreneurs will need to build partnerships across sectors in a way that Second Wave companies never had to. They will need to navigate a policy landscape that most Second Wave companies could ignore. And they will need to do it all in a space where the barriers to entry—even for a worthy idea—are far greater than anything experienced in the Second Wave.

The playbook they need, instead, is the one that worked during the First Wave, when the Internet was still young and skepticism was still high; when the barriers to entry were enormous, and when partnerships were a necessity to reaching your customers; when the regulatory system was coming to grips with a new reality and struggling to figure out the appropriate path forward.

Preface

I am writing this book today because we are living at a pivotal point in history, and I want to offer whatever perspective I can to ensure a bright future. I am writing this because the history of the First Wave has become increasingly important as a way to think about this future—how we plan for it, adapt to it, and seize upon its opportunity. And yet much of that story, including my own, remains untold.

I come to this from a variety of perspectives. As a startup entrepreneur, but with experience at a big company. As someone who's never served full-time in government but has worked in and around government. I come to this as both an investor and an advocate, and as someone who gets Silicon Valley but was never of Silicon Valley.

And so I aim to accomplish several things in this book. I want to tell you the story of how the consumer Internet was born, and how close companies like AOL came to not making it. I want to share my candid memories from behind the scenes—the details from a roller-coaster ride few have experienced. I want to tell you what it was like at the very top—and give you a view from the boardroom on the way down.

But I don't want to do any of that in a vacuum. Each of these stories is meant to illustrate a broader thesis: that the lessons from the First Wave of the Internet will be integral to the Third. And so I want to zoom in on the Third Wave as well. I'll describe what it will look like and how it will unfold, and give you a glimpse of the future it portends.

• • •

I've written this for entrepreneurs to help shape their dreams and for corporate titans to help temper their nightmares. I've written it both for the business student and the casual observer. For people old enough to feel nostalgia about AOL CDs in the mail and for those young enough never to have heard the term "CD-ROM."

My journey over the past few decades has been an unpredictable adventure, a thrilling, sometimes frustrating mix of ups and downs. It has been marked by moments of sheer terror, and many more of joy and jubilation. I've tried to convey that here. I've tried to bring you into my world. And what better medium than the book, which was invented around two thousand years ago?

I didn't want to write a memoir, but I did want to share some of my stories, as I do believe, as Shakespeare famously said, "what's past is prologue"—that there are lessons to be learned. I didn't want to write a guidebook for budding entrepreneurs, as there are plenty of those—but I did want to explain why the rules of the entrepreneurial game are changing. And I didn't want to get too wonky on policy, but I do believe America is at risk of losing its lead as the world's most entrepreneurial nation, and I wanted to explain why—and what we can and must do about it.

Writing *The Third Wave*—part memoir, part playbook for the future, part manifesto—has been a labor of love. I hope that it might light the same spark for you that Toffler's *Third Wave* lit for me.

ONE

A WINDING PATH

M Y BROTHER Dan was just thirteen months older than me, and a year ahead in school. We shared a room growing up and, like most brothers, were fairly competitive. We hated to lose. That was especially hard for me, since Dan seemed to be good at just about everything he tried. He was the more natural athlete, and always at the top of his class. When I realized I couldn't compete with him head-to-head, I tried to find interests apart from his. If he was going to play tennis, I decided, I was going to play basketball. But there was one interest we both shared that never felt like a competition. I wanted to be an entrepreneur, I was sure of it, before I even really knew what that meant. And Dan genuinely wanted to help. I got immense satisfaction from coming up with an idea, and he would revel in trying to help me turn it into something real.

We started our first business when I was ten years old. Dan was eleven, and brought to bear all of the wisdom of that extra year in our operation. We called ourselves Case Enterprises, and hoped that no one would notice that neither of us was old enough to drive. We billed ourselves as an international mail-order company. At one point we became the exclusive distributor in Hawaii for a Swiss watchmaker, though I can't recall actually selling any watches. Most of our efforts involved knocking on doors trying to sell greeting cards to our neighbors. Most of our customers were buying what we were selling just to be nice. But Dan didn't care. He called it our comparative advantage. Said it was part of our brand. We actually talked like this; our parents, a lawyer and a teacher, had no idea where we got it from. They used to joke that when I went to my room, I was going to my office.

Our early ventures may not have provided much in the way of cash, but they did provide a wealth of experience. And the process of coming up with new business ideas, or new ways to sell, left a deep impression on me. When I left Hawaii to attend Williams College in Massachusetts in 1976, I kept looking for new business opportunities. I started six little businesses while at school, including delivering fruit baskets to students during exam week (paid for by parents, of course). I had a growing interest in the music business, and spent a lot of time in New York clubs like CBGB, trying to find new talent to bring to college campuses.

I was diligent about going to class and doing my homework,

but these side businesses were my real passion. That didn't go over so well at Williams. At one point my advisor pulled me aside and suggested I was spending too much time on my entrepreneurial efforts, and would regret it. "Look at all the educational opportunities in front of you," I remember him saying. "You should immerse yourself in them. Your business pursuits are distracting, and, frankly, they are ill-suited for campus life." He wasn't alone in thinking that. I remember one of my fellow students attacking me in a school newspaper editorial. "I swore I would never go to a Steve Case party or buy a Steve Case record album," the article began. "It's nothing personal, it's just that I despise rampant laissez-faire capitalism on the college campus."

In my final year at Williams, I took an introductory computer class. I hated it—and almost flunked it. This was still the era of punch cards, where you had to write a program and then take your cards to someone to run them. Several hours later, you'd get the results—which usually (at least for me) meant finding a mistake and starting the process all over again. The tedium, and the resulting low grade, almost prevented me from graduating. And yet the experience stuck with me. The punch cards were a nuisance, but if used the right way, they could be powerful. We were building very basic computational programs, rudimentary by contemporary standards. And yet even then, the potential was obvious. Computers were solving problems in seconds that would otherwise take days, even weeks. Frustrating as it was, in retrospect, I think it was forma-tive. It was the first time I really began to grasp the potential of computers. Still, if I hadn't stumbled upon Toffler's book that year, I'm not sure I ever would have pursued the path I did.

With graduation approaching in the spring of 1980, all I could think about was breaking into the fledgling digital in-dustry. I applied for a lot of jobs, always including, with my résumé, a cover letter breathlessly predicting the dawn of a digital age.

There were few takers. Most of my letters went unanswered. On a few occasions I did get interviews, but I rarely got past the first one. People seemed put off by my musings, worried that they were getting a nutty young kid who'd never be satisfied in a normal job. As the rejections piled up, I realized that my future would require my keeping my mouth shut—at least for a time. There was not much of a startup culture then, and of course no Internet, either. If I was going to get a job and learn any useful skills, I concluded, I'd have to join a big company. I eventually accepted a job at Procter & Gamble in the brand management department. It was a great place to land, all things considered. I could learn useful skills during the day while continuing to dream about the digital world at night.

If Procter & Gamble knew one thing, it was how to make a product understandable to everyday people. When radio serials were first introduced to the public, P&G saw an op-portunity to advertise its home cleaning products to its key audience. So they began sponsoring programs, starting with

Oxydol's Own Ma Perkins back in 1933. They were known as soap operas. When the public jumped from radio to television in the 1950s, so did P&G.

The people I worked with were experts in understanding consumer preferences, doggedly pursuing R&D, and seeking breakthroughs that could give their products an edge against the competition. And they were world-class marketers, often ahead of their time. P&G was also responsible for pioneering the concept of giving away free samples to encourage trial use. (I later borrowed that idea when we launched AOL's trial program and blanketed the nation with free trial discs.)

After a couple years of working at P&G in Cincinnati, I moved to Kansas to join Pizza Hut as Director of New Pizza Development. To this day, I've never had a better title.

My motivation was twofold: First, I was offered a healthy increase in salary and responsibility, and second, I thought it would be helpful to understand how a more entrepreneurial company worked. Pizza Hut was founded in 1958 by two brothers, Dan and Frank Carney, while they were still students at Wichita State University. It had grown from a single location at the corner of Kellogg and Bluff to become the nation's largest pizza chain, which it accomplished largely by enabling franchisees to innovate. This bottom-up approach to innovation differed from P&G's top-down style, and I wanted to understand it.

Originally, the job involved my working in the test kitchens in Wichita. But I advocated that we hit the road to find out what was happening throughout the country. My view was that, though innovation was possible within our walls, most of the innovation was happening beyond them. I created and led an advance team, and we started roaming the U.S., looking for a great idea to incorporate into the new menu. The company would send me to places like Washington, DC, put me up in the Four Seasons in Georgetown, and then task me with eating the city's best pizza. There are worse ways to live. I did learn rather quickly how difficult it was to take something out of a test kitchen and then execute it across five thousand restaurants where the chefs were teenagers with limited skills. A lot of our ideas that made sense in theory flopped in practice.

At the time, one of the concepts we were testing was home delivery. This was 1982, and though pizza was popular, delivery wasn't yet universal. We were also working on ways to make pizza more convenient and more portable. We spent a lot of time trying to figure out if calzones or pocket pizzas could work as a carry-out option for people on the run. It's funny to think, looking back on that year, that the things we were focused on—convenience and portability—would become such crucial parts of the company I would later help build. So would our desire to keep things simple and focus on the basics.

I only lasted at Pizza Hut for a year. My obsession with Toffler hadn't subsided; it had intensified. I wanted to be part of his vision. I needed to find a way in.

MY FIRST STARTUP

I found my opportunity in 1982 when my brother told me about a startup called Control Video Corporation (CVC), which was trying to take the growing electronic gaming industry online. By now, Dan had moved on from CEO of Case Enterprises to up-and-coming investment banker in the Silicon Valley. Neither of us had lost that passion we first explored in childhood. I was still the ideas guy. He was still the one trying to figure out how to make it all work. When the firm he worked for, Hambrecht & Quist, was considering making an investment in CVC, Dan asked me to review the business plan and give him my impressions. I was impressed, I told him. And interested in being a part of it. H&Q did end up investing, and within months, I became a part-time consultant at CVC's headquarters in the suburbs of Washington, DC.

It was there that I met Marc Seriff, a straight-talking Texan and a brilliant engineer. He had been part of the early team that helped create the Internet in the 1970s, and he was a real visionary with incredible technical skills. Later that decade, he connected with an idea-a-minute entrepreneur, Bill von Meister, and they worked together on building a couple of companies. Von Meister had been a telecommunications pioneer, having founded one of the first online services, The Source. Along with Seriff, von Meister conceived of a business called Home Music Store. Nearly two decades before Napster (and nearly three decades before Spotify), the two were trying to offer digital music to the masses. The idea got a lot of attention in the music industry when it was announced, but they struggled to secure the rights they needed to launch. And some early supporters, like Warner Music, ended up backing out of an agreement to license music for the venture. "Delivering music directly into people's homes via satellite and cable," the Warner Music executive argued in 1981, "would completely shut out music retailers, literally choking off their money supply."

"Retailers are threatening to throw our records in the street!" he exclaimed.

It was clear that there was no budging Warner Music. But they did have a deal with Home Music Store, and they wanted to find an amicable solution. Warner Music suggested that Marc and Bill focus on using their technology to deliver video games instead. "Talk to Atari," the executive advised. "They're a division of our same parent company—Warner Communications."

So the fast-moving von Meister pivoted, and turned his attention toward building an online gaming service called GameLine. The idea was to make a game cartridge, much like Atari's, but with a cord to connect it to a phone line so you could download and play games for a monthly fee (a primitive Netflix for games).

By January 1983, Marc and Bill were fully in the video game business, and ready to announce their new service. They did so at the Consumer Electronics Show in Las Vegas, tethering a massive hot-air balloon to the roof of the Tropicana, emblazoned with the GameLine logo. I joined the company full-time nine months later, just as the product was coming to market.

It was an utter disaster.

Atari video games turned out to be a fad. After a few go-go growth years, interest in Atari products plummeted. Retailers canceled their GameLine orders. Inventory piled up. (One weekend, we quietly disposed of the tens of thousands of unsold GameLine modems in a dumpster behind our office.) GameLine's revenues were 95 percent below forecasts, so the CVC board decided to slash costs. Most of the staff lost their jobs. I went from being the youngest person on a seven-person marketing team to being the only one left in the department— mostly, I suspect, because I had the lowest salary. My parents were pretty worried. I'd had three jobs in three years, and now it looked like I would soon need another.

The experience was an early lesson in market timing and managing costs, and a valuable first experience with failure. But while GameLine's demise was agonizing and shocking, I wasn't discouraged. My hopes for GameLine had deflated, but my conviction about the digital future remained. I was confident, perhaps naïvely so, that we would figure something out.

To stave off bankruptcy, we sought partners. As an accidental senior leader in the company, I wound up with the job of striking deals wherever I could to keep the company afloat. After dozens of fruitless conversations, we finally made a deal with BellSouth, which had just recently divested from "Ma Bell" (the AT&T Corporation) after an antitrust ruling broke up the phone company. BellSouth provided some funding that kept CVC going for another year, but it became increasingly clear that our strategy of using a customized modem technology had been a mistake.

By the time we entered the market, our technology was outdated. What we'd engineered was a modem technology that was, in essence, download-only. We could send games to consumers, but consumers couldn't send much data back to us—or to one another. The modems that people were starting to purchase could do both. What we thought was CVC's core asset—a lower-cost modem technology—turned into one of its greatest liabilities. We offered a proprietary system that few wanted to adopt.

THE (FIRST) REBOOT

So we decided to abandon it and support industry-standard modem technology and the emerging personal computer market instead. We embraced the irony—a modem company with a worthless modem—and we reminded ourselves that we'd never intended to be a hardware company at all. The modem was a means to the real end: becoming a consumer online service company. So we returned to our original mission and exited the hardware business altogether. Instead, we put all of our efforts into what we were good at: crafting easy-to-use software and services that could demystify the online world.

We also decided to rethink our marketing and distribution

strategy. Rather than selling services directly to consumers, which was both costly and risky, we decided to partner with personal computer manufacturers to create private-label online services, which they in turn could sell to their customers. We'd build the software and services, they'd package and market them, and we'd share in the revenue.

In theory, it made great sense, and we were excited to get started. But as soon as we began reaching out to potential partners, we realized we had a problem. We kept getting brushed off. Some thought the appeal of getting online would be limited. And those who sensed the potential were unwilling to take the risk of partnering with a young company, particularly one that had a failed product and angry creditors and investors.

We finally found a willing ear at Commodore, at the time one of the leading home computer companies. Commodore's founder had departed in a huff, and the remaining management team was struggling to figure out a path forward. Competition was intensifying, and they knew they needed a new act, an angle that would allow them to stand out.

Commodore's head of strategic planning, Clive Smith, was willing to be our advocate, but other executives had concluded it would be too risky to partner with CVC.

"You guys have a ton of baggage and it's a liability for us," Clive said, without pulling any punches. "Everyone has a lot of respect for what you guys are trying to do here, but no one wants to get in bed with CVC. There's just too much risk."

I asked him for advice. Was there anything we could do to get around it? Any chance for a second shot? There was a silence on the other end of the phone. We were doomed, I was sure of it, and he just didn't know how to say it.

"I don't know, Steve," he finally responded. "Have you thought about starting a new company?"

Oddly, I hadn't. And yet it seemed so obvious once he said it. A new company would mean more than just a new name. It would mean a clean balance sheet and a clean slate. A genuine fresh start. All we'd need to do was license the software from CVC, move the team over to the new company, and dissolve the old one.

In the summer of 1985, just before my twenty-seventh birthday, we took Clive's advice and created a new company, Quantum Computer Services. We took over the lease on CVC's office space in Tysons Corner, Virginia, and hired most of its team. I joined together with Marc Seriff and Jim Kimsey, another CVC executive, as one of Quantum's co-founders.

Jim was a truly colorful character. Like many of us, he had come to the company with no professional background in technology. He owned a group of bars and restaurants in Washington, DC, and had a lifestyle to match. A graduate of West Point and a veteran of two tours in Vietnam, Jim often laced his sentences with expletives and non sequiturs. He had a thing for quoting historical figures. Nietzsche was a favorite; I must have heard him say "if it doesn't kill you, it makes you stronger" at least a hundred times. He was twenty years older than most of us and, to the outside world, was clearly seen as the adult in the mix. Our investors referred to him as our "adult supervision." This served an important purpose in those days, when companies with twenty-somethings hadn't yet established themselves as a force.

Frank Caufield, one of Jim's best friends and the co-founder of a young venture capital firm called Kleiner Perkins Caufield Byers (KPCB), had talked to Jim about CVC. Jim got excited about the GameLine vision and bought the franchise rights for the DC region. When KPCB joined H&Q as early investors in CVC, Frank joined the board. When problems emerged with GameLine, Frank asked Jim to step in to try to stabilize the situation and protect KPCB's investment. Jim agreed to help, even though he didn't really understand technology—and didn't really want to. He viewed it as more of an interim stint, figuring he'd help out for a few months as a favor. He ended up doing it for more than a decade.

Without Jim, we wouldn't have had the ability to raise the capital to survive. And without Marc, we wouldn't have been able to build the core technology of our product. I played the role of the strategist and hustler, coming up with the ideas, building partnerships, designing many of the consumer-facing aspects of the product, and handling our branding and message. It was the perfect combination of highly complementary skills. And we hoped it would make us a credible bet—particularly because we needed to raise some capital if we were going to pull off the pivot.

. . .

We met with our CVC investors and pitched them the plan. They were intrigued but remained skeptical of us. Having just lost their money on our previous effort, they expected a much bigger stake if they were going to take another leap with our team. They didn't just want to generate a return on their new capital; they were also looking for a payback on their squandered investment. We didn't want to give up so much of the company, but we knew we had very little choice. In 1985, the startup tech world was still young, and venture investors were hard to come by. If we couldn't get a deal here, we were going to go out of business.

Our investors had all the leverage, and they used it to their advantage. They crafted a deal wherein they would own virtually all of the company, allowing management to earn some of it back over time, depending on our performance. All told, I don't think I ever owned more than 3 percent. But it didn't matter. It had never been about the money, anyway. It was always about the vision. I didn't like the deal the investors imposed on us, but I was happy to keep the idea alive—and delighted to have another shot at building a business.

We were able to launch Quantum with just a million dollars of new capital, largely because we were able to leverage partnerships to minimize our marketing costs. We customized our pitch for each PC company, and we started small. First we struck a deal with Commodore to create a gaming-centric service called Q-Link for their vast base of Commodore 64 computer users. That helped us negotiate a partnership with RadioShack to create PC-Link, a downloading service that leveraged their graphical user interface. We later convinced IBM to partner with us to create an educational service called Promenade. Each company had its own unique brand and tailored offering, but their online services would all be built and run by us.

This time it worked. We kept costs low and were able to achieve profitability in our second year of business. And while growth was modest, it was steady. We believed that the best way to jump-start our growth was to secure a major partnership—so we set our sights on Apple.

THE KINGS OF CUPERTINO

I rented an apartment in San Francisco in 1987 and showed up at Apple's headquarters every day—for six months. I buttonholed everybody I could within Apple to try to interest them in the nascent online market. I would tailor my pitch, depending on which team I was talking to, trying to come up with the perfect reason for them to partner with us. Ultimately, the group that was most interested was probably the group that had the least power and influence within the company: the customer service group.

My pitch to them was straightforward: If you launch this service and bundle it with your computers, it'll be a cheaper, better way to provide customer service to Apple customers than staffing large call centers to handle phone calls. "Oh, and by the way," I would add, "in addition to the customer service benefit, we can provide a suite of other services that will make it compelling for consumers and help differentiate Apple."

The pitch resonated well with them. The people I was dealing with saw it as a way to be strategic, to strengthen their position within the company. On the one hand, they knew that their involvement was predicated on the partnership's being about customer support. But they also saw that there was a broader opportunity—and that if online services took off, this was something that could transform their customer service department from being a drain to a profit center. A career-accelerating move, to be sure. So we seemed equally motivated to make the partnership work.

Had Steve Jobs been at Apple at the time, I suspect the deal would never have happened. Steve never would have licensed the Apple name or allowed such a critical decision to be made by lower-level executives. But Steve had been fired by Apple a couple of years earlier, so we had an opening. Six months after I'd moved to San Francisco, we finally inked a deal to build the service. It would be called AppleLink Personal Edition.

I moved back to DC, where the team greeted me like a conquering hero. Securing a partnership with Apple and convincing them to license their brand name to us was a coup. With Apple's commitment and endorsement, we were able to bring in a $5 million round of funding—the most we had ever raised. We opened a Cupertino office not far from Apple's headquarters so that our people could work in close collaboration with theirs. And we ramped up hiring to handle the Apple launch, which was going to be our biggest ever.

Once the early software prototype was ready, I had the chance to sit down with Alan Kay, one of the pioneers of the early computing era, to get his advice. In the 1970s, Kay was part of the team at Xerox PARC (Palo Alto Research Center) responsible for designing a programming language called Smalltalk, which could be used to network computers together and would later help inspire Apple's early Macintosh computers. When I met with him, he was working as an Apple Fellow, living in Los Angeles. I flew down to get his take on our design and to ask for guidance in making the software more intuitive, something that was his—and Apple's—specialty. It was an honor to sit with such a legend. But it would turn out to be one of the very few good days I had working with Apple. The honeymoon was short-lived.

We spent a year building the AppleLink service, and geared up for an ambitious (and expensive) launch. But from the beginning, our companies clashed. Apple wanted to sell the software and limit distribution to authorized Apple stores. We thought that approach was a terrible idea and ran counter to our whole strategy. We wanted to give the software away for free—in a wide range of retail stores, pre-installed on Apple computers, bundled with magazines and modems, and sent by mail. We wanted to make the initial trial free, too, so that it would be easier to convince people to try the service. We needed paying customers—but that meant making it as easy as possible for consumers to try us. (It's ironic that two decades later, Apple's success would be propelled by free software in their App Store.) We argued bitterly for months, battling over various marketing approaches, without ever finding common ground. It bred frustration and distrust, and a growing skepticism inside Apple.

I was late to the office one morning; there'd been an accident near Dulles Airport, and traffic was backed up for miles. When I arrived, there was a note from my assistant on my desk marked "urgent." A senior executive at Apple wanted to speak to me, she said, and he didn't sound happy. On its face, there was nothing that unusual about the message. We'd been arguing with Apple for months, and I'd gotten an earful from plenty of their executives. I didn't realize they'd be asking for a divorce.

"Listen, Case, bottom line is this," the executive said sharply, when I finally called him back. "This was a mistake, and we need to cancel the deal. We're out. It's over." I tried to change his mind, to see if there was any alternative, but even as the words came out, I knew it was futile. We were never going to see eye to eye on strategy, and each was convinced the other was wrong.

It was over. Really over. And none of us had any idea what to do.

TWO

GETTING AMERICA ONLINE

I SAT SILENTLY at my desk after I hung up the phone. I don't think I budged for an hour. I had no idea what to do, and I didn't want to break the news to the others until I had some semblance of a plan. But what possible plan was there? Our whole strategy had been to team up with computer manufacturers, but now we were without Apple, our largest and most important partner. At some point, I had to just get up and alert the others. I gathered the troops in our conference room. It was like going through the five stages of grief all in the same afternoon.

First, denial. Marc was convinced the deal wasn't really dead, that this was just a bluff in a game of poker we'd been playing for months. Then came anger, first at Apple, then each other. "Why did we have to be so goddamn rigid?" Jim yelled, looking straight at me. "We can't expect to work with partners

27

and get everything we want. It doesn't work like that!" Then came bargaining. I stood at a whiteboard and wrote out a list of concessions we could offer Apple to get the deal back on track. Everyone called out suggestions. But by the time we were done putting the list together, we realized that none of us were really willing to make those kinds of sacrifices. "If we do it Apple's way, we will fail," I said. "But if we lose Apple, we could lose our investors. At the same time, I don't know how we can make an offer like this and then look at our investors with a straight face. What's the point of continuing on a path that's going to fail?"

That's when the depression set in. I couldn't imagine how uncomfortable the next board meeting would be. Our investors had already taken a flier on us—twice. And several had pushed Jim to fire me for spending too much on the Apple launch. This surely would be the final straw.

We sat silently in the room, disappointed, frustrated, and fearful. We were at the end of the line, it seemed, and no one wanted to be the one to say so. Jim finally broke the silence.

"Here's what we have to do, guys. Apple can't just unilaterally cancel the agreement. We raised and spent millions to support the AppleLink launch. We need to threaten to sue them, and force them to pay us a settlement. Then we can use that money to stay alive until we figure out our next move."

The next move was really the only move we could make. It was both obvious and terrifying. "We have to move beyond the private label strategy," I said. "We need to create our own brand, propelled by our own marketing, paid for by us. Let's combine all of our independent separate services—Q-Link, PC-Link, AppleLink, and Promenade—into one service."

"Do we even have the runway for that?" asked Marc.

"No, but we need to find a way to raise the money to make the transition," I said. "And the first place to focus is on getting as much money from Apple as we can. If they want a divorce, so be it. But they need to pay for it, so we can move ahead on our own."

I left the room and went back to my office to reread the agreement we had signed with Apple. I jotted down all the commitments they had made that they were now reneging on. I huddled with Jim to figure out a plan. Then we took a deep breath and hit redial on my phone.

We told the Apple executive that we didn't want protracted litigation over the breach of contract, that it wasn't in either of our best interests to go down that road. And so we suggested a settlement: For a onetime payment of $5 million—the amount our venture capitalists had kicked in to support the Apple deal—we'd agree to void the contract. Otherwise, we'd file suit, and be noisy about how bad a partner Apple had been.

The response was tentative. The $5 million demand was rejected, but it was clear Apple recognized that they had culpability and liability and would pay us something to go away quietly. After a few weeks of back-and-forth and several trips to California, we finally struck a deal. Apple would pay us $3 million to tear up the contract. We'd stop using the Apple brand and go our separate ways.

Just a few years after pivoting from CVC to Quantum, we were once again starting over, this time with Apple's cash. Our team rallied, working endless hours to make the new vision a reality. It felt, at times, like a moonshot. But it was ours, and we weren't going to stop until we got it right—or ran out of money trying.

By then, our team's mood had brightened. Fear was replaced by relief. Apple was a difficult, demanding partner, and for months we had been dealing with one crisis after another. Once the shock had passed and acceptance kicked in, people got back to work, filled with excitement about what we might build.

We had the chance to become the direct portal to an online world for everyone with a modem. It was a long shot—but what if it worked?

We didn't know what to call it, and couldn't afford to hire a branding firm. So we held an internal competition with our employees and debated the options for weeks. The leading choice was Online America, which most people generally liked but which never struck my ear the right way. "How about we flip it? America Online," I suggested. It stuck. We renamed the service (and later the company) and suited up for launch.

A DIZZYING TRANSITION

The rollout of the AOL service was a little bumpy. Users had different computers and somewhat different needs, so it took us nearly a year before we got much traction. Our growth finally accelerated once we launched the Windows version. We were suddenly picking up users at a rapid clip, and they seemed to love our service. The press was intrigued as well; our coverage was wonderful. We were the underdog startup, fighting the big, entrenched companies. And we had a better sense of what consumers wanted, because we were living and breathing the service, not just relying on focus group research.

One afternoon, I was chatting with some of our employees at AOL's headquarters in Tysons Corner about trying to make the software feel a little more friendly and accessible. There were still plenty of online skeptics, plenty of people who couldn't understand what the Internet would offer them. It all seemed too impersonal, too detached from genuine social interaction. I knew that was wrong, both from my own experience and from that of our happy customers. AOL wasn't limiting social interaction; it was magnifying it, making it possible to communicate to more people in more ways than at any time in human history. But we needed to listen to the concerns of the unconverted so that we could convince them to give AOL a try.

I had an idea. Why not make the service more personal by adding the voice of a person? Karen Edwards, one of the customer service team members, overheard me make the suggestion.

"If you need help with that, my husband, Elwood, does

voice-overs," she told me. "He's done a bunch of radio commercials."

I'd never met him, and didn't know what his voice sounded like. But I figured it would at least be a good prototype, a sample we could play for other voice-over actors when we started auditions. So I scribbled a few phrases onto a Post-it note and handed them to Karen.

"See if he's interested in recording these for us. Think he could get it done by the end of the week?"

"He'll do it tonight," she said. "I'll make sure of it!"

The next day she brought the recordings to me. His voice couldn't have been more perfect. It was disarmingly friendly, like the voice you'd expect from a stranger who offered to carry your grandmother's groceries. The second I heard it, I knew we weren't going to be auditioning anyone else. I instructed our engineers to add the voice files to the new version of our software.

Within a month, we were mailing CDs to millions of Americans, each containing our upgraded software and a message from Elwood.

"Welcome. . . . You've got mail."

You could feel the excitement in the office as it became clear our pivot had been successful. The fear of going under had subsided, and our team was genuinely enthusiastic about our future prospects. After many years and several false starts, we had finally found our footing.

In the process, I emerged as the company's leader. People

appreciated the critical roles Jim and Marc had played to get us going, but the team increasingly looked to me for guidance. In January 1991, the board voted to make me the CEO. I was thirty-two.

My key focus was expanding our customer base. We knew tough competition was coming, so I pushed the team to go faster and grow faster. "It will never be easier or cheaper to gain market share" became my mantra. We slammed on the accelerator, dramatically increasing our marketing spending.

To raise money to fuel this rapid expansion, in late 1991 we decided we needed to take our company public. The board concurred, but there was a catch. America Online would be the first Internet company to go public. The market size was unclear, and the competitive risks significant. So the board quietly huddled and decided to reverse the CEO decision. They concluded that I was too young to be accepted by institutional investors who were used to much older CEOs.

Jim took me to lunch to break the news. "Everybody thinks you're doing a great job," he assured me, "but you're young and untested, and most companies going public have much older CEOs who have long track records. So I need to step back in as CEO. You need to go back to being executive vice president.

"Don't worry," Jim told me, "it's only temporary."

I was devastated. Furious. I felt like I'd been robbed. I wasn't an accidental CEO. I had earned the job painstakingly over time. And to be sidelined, not because of my skills, but because of a theoretical fear that investors would be skittish about my age—it all seemed totally preposterous to me. I thought about quitting. And when others on the team learned of the board's decision, many offered to resign in protest. I was heartened by the support, but I knew that I couldn't leave the company, and couldn't let anybody else leave, either. I'd invested too much of myself into it—and so had they. So I let my dissatisfaction be known but ultimately chose to suck it up and stay.

GOING PUBLIC

In March 1992 we went public. At the time, we had fewer than 200 employees and a mere 184,000 subscribers. We had $30 million in revenue and had raised a total of $10 million over the previous seven years. We raised an additional $10 million in the initial public offering, at a $70 million valuation. Most institutional investors weren't particularly interested in us, seeing us as a small player in a niche market. The *Wall Street Journal* didn't even call AOL an "Internet company" or a "tech company"; in describing our IPO, they called us a "computer-based provider of consumer services."

But the ride was just beginning. The IPO gave us not only capital to expand but also public visibility and a currency (stock value) that we could use for acquisitions. It also gave individual investors—ordinary citizens—the chance to be part of a fast-growing company, something that is all too rare today.

Our first post-IPO acquisition came to our attention through my brother. Ted Leonsis, the thirty-five-year-old

CEO of Redgate Communications, had hired Dan's firm to represent him in a transaction. The two got to talking and Dan suggested he introduce us. "You guys should really meet," Dan said, "because you're talking about the exact same stuff." When my brother called me to set up the meeting, I told him that I'd already heard of Ted.

Ted was at the forefront of a lot of early digital innovation. He had been as taken as I was by the possibilities that the Internet offered. Ted once told the *New York Times* that "in '84 and '85, no matter what meeting I was in, I felt something cataclysmic was happening." I could relate.

At Redgate, Ted produced some of the first multimedia CD-ROMs, as well as a pioneering shopping service (we didn't yet call it ecommerce) that used graphics stored on disks to create a compelling visual buying experience (keep in mind, at the time most online services were text-centric). He had written three books and started half a dozen magazines focused on technology. What had gotten my attention, in particular, was Ted's seemingly innate ability to envision and evangelize a digital future, something I was very focused on doing with AOL. So before I even sat down for breakfast with Ted, I was eager to make a move.

We had a warm and engaging conversation that lasted about ninety minutes. He was very impressive. After the waitress dropped off our check, I decided it was time to make an offer.

"I want you on our team," I told him. "We'd be great together."

"We probably would," he responded, "and I'm flattered. But I love what I'm doing at Redgate and I couldn't walk away from the company."

"Ted, you misunderstand. I'm not here just to offer you a job. I want to buy your company."

Ted has a great poker face, and he was careful to be non-committal.

"Can we date first?" he asked.

But I knew I had him. Our visions were too similar for him to say no. I knew that what was coming out of his mouth belied what was going on behind those eyes. He was imagining what it would be like to use his skills on the biggest possible stage. It was only a matter of time.

Ted became one of AOL's most influential executives. A few months after we closed on the acquisition of Florida-based Redgate, Ted agreed to move to the DC area to oversee the AOL service. Later, we put him in charge of our content efforts, where he acquired brands like Moviefone, created the Digital Cities local brand in partnership with newspapers, and launched one of the Internet's first incubator and accelerator programs, called AOL Greenhouse. The strategy was to help develop new brands, then launch them with independent management teams and outside investors. The goal was to let them be nimble, while leveraging the AOL platform. Greenhouse helped launch dozens of brands, including The Motley Fool, a personal finance software, and PlanetOut, an LGBT-focused digital media company founded by Megan Smith, who later become an early Google executive and, later still, White House's chief technology officer.

Seven months after our IPO, Walt Mossberg, a highly influential and widely read technology columnist then writing for the *Wall Street Journal*, penned a glowing review of our service, comparing us favorably to our biggest competitor:

> Prodigy is huge, claiming 1,750,000 subscribers, but it has been aimed mainly at computer novices. It is taking some welcome steps to become speedier and more sophisticated. But at present I regard Prodigy as seriously flawed. Its navigation system is unusual and confusing, its text is clunky and moves at a snail's pace, its content promises more than it delivers. And the service splashes distracting paid advertisements across the bottom of many of the information screens (including pitches for this newspaper and even for America Online).
>
> In contrast, I see America Online as the sophisticated wave of the future among such services. Though it has just 200,000 subscribers and still suffers from some shortcomings, America Online features the type of graphical user interface, popularized by the Apple Macintosh and Microsoft Windows on the PC, that is sweeping all of personal computing. It uses overlapping windows to hold and display text that can be freely manipulated, menus

of plain-English commands that can be selected with the mouse, and colorful icons you can click to quickly reach any of a wide variety of rich information databases.

That review was a tipping point in terms of how people viewed the online market. They took it—and us—a lot more seriously. We were still small; but now we were on the map. And our growth accelerated from there.

In the spring of 1993, Jim and I went to lunch a short drive from our headquarters. When the waiter came over, Jim ordered a bottle of champagne, the nicest on the menu.

"Are we celebrating something?" I asked.

"We sure are," he said.

"Okay," I said, with confusion in my voice. "What is it we're celebrating?"

"You," he said.

"Why me?"

"Because I'm stepping down and you're stepping up."

The waiter popped the cork and poured two glasses.

"You see," Jim said, holding his up to toast. "I told you it would only be temporary."

The board voted me back in as CEO. Over the next three years we grew to 4,000 employees and were creating 200 jobs each month. Within seven years, we had 25 million customers and were one of the most highly valued companies in the world.

For those of you who don't remember or who weren't old enough, it may be hard to appreciate how significant AOL's role was in ushering in the Internet age. But in the late 1990s, AOL was the way most people did everything there was to do online. If you were online then, the odds are high that the first time you connected to the Internet, the first time you sent an email, the first time you did a search, the first time you received electronic news, the first time you bought anything online, the first time you heard music or watched a video online, the first time you saw, sent, or stored photos online, the first time you connected with friends online, it happened on AOL. For most Americans, AOL was, for its time, Google, Facebook, Twitter, Amazon, Spotify, YouTube, and Instagram combined.

AOL wasn't the first service to connect people to the Internet, but we were the first to turn the Internet into a way of life. We were the first to allow millions of people to instant message with friends. We were the first to offer a complete shopping mall, anchored by major retailers. We were the first to partner with dozens of magazines and newspapers, kick-starting the dramatic transformation of the way journalists create and people consume their news. We were proud of these innovations. But at the core, what we built, and cultivated, was the first widespread online community.

I saw my role at AOL, in addition to my being CEO, as that of mayor of the online community we built. I was trying to get people comfortable with this new digital medium, trying to put a friendly—and human—face on it. In some cases, that meant small things, like the monthly letters I wrote to members for more than a decade, updating people on what we were doing, and highlighting new features. In others, it meant being the public face of a crisis while trying to solve it from behind the scenes.

I remember one early morning phone call particularly well.

"There's a problem. We're down," Mike Connors, a buttoned-up IBM executive who had recently become the leader of AOL's technology and operations team, said. "The whole site is down. Nobody can log in. Customer service is overloaded with calls from customers complaining. And it may take us a while to fix it."

It was August 7, 1996, just a little more than four years after we'd gone public.[1] AOL system administrators had just completed a code push, updating our software to cope with our growth. We had shifted from charging customers for the hours they spent on AOL to charging a flat rate fee for un-limited access. As a result, usage was soaring; we had added more than 1 million new users in the six months leading up to that morning.[2]

For our customers, there was no way to figure out what was wrong by checking out Twitter. There was no Google yet. Newspapers were still printing the word "email" with a hyphen and quotes around it, followed by a description of what it was. The World Wide Web was still a new concept. For most people, AOL represented their entire experience with the Internet.

At the time, AOL was the dominant Internet provider, han-dling nearly half of all U.S. traffic. So whereas today, when a service like Snapchat goes down, it creates a lot of annoyance, back in 1996, when AOL went down, it caused a national incident.

As the hours ticked on, the complaints flooded in. We got phone calls from consumers and companies that were paralyzed without access to email. A swarm of frantic engineers tried to isolate and fix the problem. But twelve hours in, the problem still wasn't resolved. The story of AOL's being down led the network TV news shows and was a front-page headline in almost every newspaper in the country. I did dozens of interviews, trying to explain how such a calamity could have happened—and when it might be resolved. In the end it took us twenty-three hours to get our systems back online.

It was a bizarre experience, and an incredible realization, all at the same time. After years of evangelizing the benefits of going online to an audience that rarely seemed convinced, watching the commotion was surreal. On the one hand, we had been under siege, trying to calm people down while we worked feverishly to get things back online. On the other, we felt this sense of excitement. What better proof that the Internet had entered the mainstream? Finally, after more than a decade of struggling, the Internet's First Wave was gaining momentum.

THREE

THE THIRD WAVE

I T MIGHT seem that the lessons from the First Wave of the Internet are ancient. Outdated. Of little use to the contemporary entrepreneur. But that misunderstands what is old about the story. It is true, of course, that technology has made tremendous strides since those early days, when we had to get online with rudimentary Apple II computers, via maddeningly slow 300-baud modems. And yet, even with the most modern technology, the entrepreneurs of the Third Wave will spend a great deal of time focused on things other than tech. They will need a strategy—just as we did—to build an Internet infrastructure in skeptical industries with powerful gatekeepers. Where we worked to make connections to the Internet itself, they will work on connecting the Internet to everything else. And in critical ways, their experience is going to be more analogous to the First Wave than to the second.

During the Second Wave, the surge in Internet usage, coupled with the rapid adoption of smartphones, led to an explosion in social media and the creation of a thriving app economy. Some of the most successful companies, such as Snapchat and Twitter, started with small engineering teams and became overnight sensations, requiring none of the partnerships and perseverance that had come to define the previous era.

But there are signs that this model is now peaking, that a new wave is about to break. And there is growing evidence that this new period will look quite different from the Second Wave—and quite similar to the First.

The Third Wave of the Internet will be defined not by the Internet of Things; it will be defined by the Internet of Everything. We are entering a new phase of technological evolution, a phase where the Internet will be fully integrated into every part of our lives—how we learn, how we heal, how we manage our finances, how we get around, how we work, even what we eat. As the Third Wave gains momentum, every industry leader in every economic sector is at risk of being disrupted. Think about what's been happening in Silicon Valley over the past few decades and imagine what it will look like when we apply that same culture of innovation and scope of ambition to every part of our economy. That's the Third Wave—and it's not just coming; it's here.

A HEALTHY HEALTHCARE SYSTEM

ıı ر۔۔ ı tech entrepreneur looking for an industry to disrupt, what better place to begin than the healthcare system? For starters, it's massive—making up one-sixth of the U.S. economy. On top of that, healthcare industry incumbents have been disturbingly slow in the adoption of technology. As most can attest, going to a hospital often feels like you're stepping back in time. Many hospitals still use paper medical records and fax machines. Most can't even tell you what their services cost. And most research and development is focused on medical devices and pharmaceuticals, with very little focus on how to use connected technology to improve outcomes. The lack of coordination and actionable data makes for a tenuous healthcare system, riddled with error. As patients, we are expected to seek expensive second opinions, not because insurance companies want us to but because misdiagnosis is disconcertingly common. In September 2011, for example, MD Anderson researchers found that as much as 25 percent of the time, a second opinion results in a change of diagnosis.

And yet for decades, complacency has been held up like a value to behold. If you've ever wondered why the American healthcare system costs more than other advanced countries' but doesn't produce better results, this is why. Our hospitals are stuck in a pre-Internet world, and patients are suffering because of it.

Luckily, entrepreneurs see an opportunity. In 2014, digital health startups raised four times as much money as they had in

2010. What began with fitness trackers that measure steps and speed and heart rate will soon transform into hardware and software that will enable users to take the full range of vital signs on a serial basis, collecting and saving data and alerting patients and their doctors if something is wrong. It won't be long before tracking your vitals on a daily basis will become routine, as simple and essential as brushing your teeth. It may sound basic, but it will have profound effects both on how patients are treated as individuals and on how the entire health system operates.

When your doctor receives a summary of your health tracking data, she's leveraging a tool of precision that she currently lacks. Today, when a doctor asks us questions like "When did it start bothering you?" or "Have you noticed any other symptoms?," too often, we don't have an accurate answer to provide. In most cases, that lack of precision may not be significant, but there are times when a more accurate reading could be the difference between life and death. It can give a doctor the tools to assess whether the headache a patient is complaining about is a simple migraine or a deadly aneurysm—perhaps before the patient even arrives at the hospital. It means being warned, at home, by your smartphone, of the clot before the stroke or the clog before the heart attack—a warning that will make your mobile device seem smarter and more essential than ever.

This kind of technology can also help reduce disease mismanagement, which accounts for more than 30 percent of healthcare spending. With connected devices, doctors will be able to monitor high-risk patients at home, using sensors that check everything from a patient's vitals to whether she's taking the right medications at the right time. These kinds of innovations could save tens of thousands of lives each year while substantially bringing down healthcare costs.

Of course, in the Third Wave, it won't just be doctors who analyze your health data; it will be third-party apps designed to keep you healthy. Imagine the possibility of instant diagnosis, not by a doctor, but by a supercomputer like IBM's Watson. These are the kinds of changes that will reverberate throughout the entire healthcare system. The CDC estimates that 200,000 people each year suffer preventable deaths from chronic disease. What if getting them to the hospital a day or even an hour earlier could save their lives? We can even quantify the value of those better outcomes: According to the consulting firm McKinsey, the value to the economy of this kind of monitoring could be as much as $1 trillion per year by 2025.[1] And that's before we even begin to look at the data in the aggregate. Once researchers have access to anonymous population-wide data, once that data can be analyzed, we'll be able to see once-invisible patterns. That could change everything from how we track epidemics to how we characterize illnesses themselves, driving a genuine revolution in medicine.

TRANSFORMING EDUCATION

More personal. More individualized. More data-driven. This is not just the mantra of the healthcare system's future. It is the mantra of the entire Third Wave. And it applies to another system that is big, important, complicated, and broken: the American education system.

Third Wave organizations—both for-profit and nonprofit—will leverage technology to revolutionize the way we learn. During the First and Second Waves, technology in the classroom looked a lot like technology outside of it: students at computers, making PowerPoint decks, browsing the web, chatting with virtual pen pals on the other side of the world. Each of these tools has proved useful, but few of them were designed specifically for the classroom. During the Third Wave, that is beginning to change.

Already, there are tools that teachers can use to interact with parents in ways that would have been inconceivable twenty years ago. Many schools now use virtual dashboards, where teachers post everything from homework assignments and test scores to videos of your child reading a book report in front of the class. Rather than reducing children to numbers, this kind of technology can provide a vehicle for parental involvement that didn't exist before.

There are also new tools for teachers and students. In 2015, for example, I invested in Pear Deck, an Iowa-based startup that allows teachers to share interactive slide decks with their students in real time, while enabling students to indicate to teachers when they are having trouble, so that the teachers can adjust. There are also emerging Internet platforms where course materials can be shared and reviewed. In 2015, the *New York Times* reported on a company called Teachers Pay Teachers, which provides an online marketplace where teachers can buy and sell lesson plans. One teacher profiled generated about $100,000 in revenue from a year's worth of grammar, vocabulary, and literature exercises. "What started out as a hobby has turned into a business," she told the *Times*. Teachers Pay Teachers CEO Alan Freed told the newspaper that twelve teachers on the site have become millionaires. "If you have a kid in school in America, they are interacting somewhere with Teachers Pay Teachers' content," said Freed.

Companies are also designing technologies to personalize the learning process—software that adapts based on how a student learns best. Students of the not-too-distant future might have the equivalent of a virtual tutor, a textbook replaced by tablets that track not only whether a child is learning but how he learns best. As the "textbook" gets smarter, so will the student's teacher, who will have tools to leverage the data, and the time to work with students in the classroom one-on-one. Teachers will create short, targeted interventions that keep students on track or provide opportunities for them to go deeper in areas of interest and strength. The key will be replacing a culture of standardization with a culture of personalization. We don't all learn the same way, or at the same pace—so why should we all be taught the same way?

Third Wave technology will also change how we measure success in the classroom. What good is an annual standardized test, after all, once teachers and parents can get detailed reports with a wide range of metrics, comparing their students

on a regular basis to others in their class or school o.
this way, big data on individual students will do for ea
what standardized testing never quite could: bring quant. .e
precision to a qualitative learning process.

Over time, the role of the teacher may be transformed as well. In the mold of programs like Khan Academy, students may start streaming lectures at home on their textbook tablet, then spend class time doing what used to be called "homework." Instead of giving a one-size-fits-all lecture to thirty students of varying levels of achievement, teachers could roam the classroom while students are working on problems, intervening to help them overcome barriers in the lesson. In the future, we may not be judging our children's classes by their size but by the number of minutes they get to work one-on-one with their teacher each day—and by their actual learning progress. This would also allow us to stop using the blunt instruments of race or income to describe and address achievement gaps, and to focus instead on ensuring that each child's personalized needs are met.

Whether that model will produce better outcomes for students remains an open question. But it's one that can be answered by the data it helps us collect. We'll suddenly have the ability to run low-cost experiments to figure out the effectiveness of these programs—in real time. It's as easy as piloting the program in one classroom and comparing the outcomes to another classroom. Does the model work? The data can increasingly tell us, potentially very quickly. A school won't have to wait until the end of a long, expensive, multiyear evaluation to decide whether they are helping or harming students with this new model. They can adopt successful plans and techniques school-wide. And they can abandon unsuccessful pilots before they do harm.

Herein lies the transformative value of integrating the Third Wave into education. Today, the barriers for innovation in the field are high. And it's not just because of government. Look at just about any public or private school in the country and you'll see a structure that has barely changed since the nineteenth century. Talk to education reformers and they will tell you that one of the chief challenges they face is an education system that is extremely cautious. People are often more worried about the risk of trying something new than about the risk of maintaining the status quo. And too often, the latter wins out. The Third Wave won't solve this problem altogether, but it can help. It can answer questions we've never had answers for, explain patterns we never would have seen on our own, and solve problems we didn't even know we had.

Ultimately, the reinvention of education will require a multifaceted approach. Of course, at the core is the material that is being learned—the content, if you will. But, as we saw in the early days of AOL, it's a mistake to focus solely on content. In the First Wave, we learned that context and community were equally important. At AOL, context meant packaging and curating to help guide people through a seemingly endless array of options, and striking deals with media companies that had trusted brands in order to help attract a mainstream audience.

And community meant creating ways for people to connect with the content, and with each other. Those same "3 C's" that drove AOL's success in the First Wave—content, context, and community—will likely power the education revolution in the Third Wave. Yes, you need teachers presenting content in the right way. But you can't stop there. You also need respected brands (for example, top universities) offering credentials (degrees, or badges) that employers will value. And, you need to create communities around the content so that students can learn from each other, and then have a lifelong relationship with each other, forming a network that persists long after graduation. Education innovators were often too focused on technology in the First Wave, and too much on content in the Second Wave. The winners in the Third Wave will leverage technology and focus on great content, but also understand the importance of context and community. The integrated approaches they bring to market, largely in partnership with others, will likely usher in the revolution in learning that has been talked about for decades, but has yet to bear much fruit.

THE FUTURE OF FOOD

The food industry is a $5 trillion sector, and, unless you grow your own vegetables and hunt your own game, chances are you're a frequent customer. Any Third Wave entrepreneur would look at those numbers and see opportunity. A lot of people have—and a lot of people do. They see a chance for innovative Third Wave companies to challenge the way food is produced, distributed, and consumed.

That doesn't mean you should expect to start seeing edible microchips. The only apples with Wi-Fi connections will still be your iPhone or MacBook. It also doesn't mean you should expect mainstream adoption of "food alternatives" such as Soylent, a powder mixed with water that's popular among some Silicon Valley elites.

Instead, the Third Wave will fundamentally change how we grow and raise our food, how we store it and transport it safely, and how we deliver it to customers.

Out of necessity, the agriculture industry has long embraced technological advances as a way to improve productivity and cut costs. Farms across America have, for years, been using sensors to track temperature, water saturation, and other critical variables for healthy yields of fruits and vegetables. But the Third Wave will take that to a whole new level. As reporter Nicole Kobie explained in the *Guardian*, the Third Wave may even save the bee population, which has been dying off mysteriously for years, creating a threat to our ability to pollinate our fields. One of the primary causes of the collapse of bee colonies is the presence of a particular type of mite. These mites can be killed by heat, but heating up the hive will melt the wax it's made of. Killing mites that way would take out the bees, too.

So a group of researchers set out to solve the problem, developing a way "to heat up specific spots in a hive from the inside, rather than heating the entire structure, using circuitry that's screen-printed on to a hive base, called a foundation," Kobie wrote. The bees build their home following the screen-printed pattern, creating a colony that's connected directly to the Internet. Will MacHugh, one of the lead researchers, explained the system to Kobie: "What our electronics do is two things: they monitor temperature and they produce heat." When the sensors detect a bee larva that might be susceptible to a mite, they heat up the area around it, killing any nearby attackers without harming the larva or weakening the hive structure.

"The bees actually kind of like it," said MacHugh. "The mites, because they're so much smaller, it almost pops them like popcorn."

Once produce is harvested and livestock slaughtered, food in America goes through a food safety system that was created by Teddy Roosevelt a century ago and hasn't changed that much since. In most processing plants, inspectors from the USDA look at less than 1 percent of the meat being processed. And the inspections they do conduct are mostly done by sight. Even when they test for foodborne pathogens, a positive result for something as dangerous as salmonella rarely shuts down an operation. From a public health perspective, food safety needs a technological reboot.

Third Wave entrepreneurs are poised to revolutionize this process. There are companies, for example, working on ways to use beams of light to kill pathogens without heating up meat, making it possible to guarantee safe processing rather than just spot-checking it. There are others working on smart

packaging—embedded with RFID (radio-frequency iden-
tification), NFC (near field communication), or Bluetooth
technology. This will allow constant real-time monitoring of
meat, making sure that refrigeration remains constant from
factory to refrigerator.

It won't be long before we can take this technological evolution one step further. Imagine a refrigerator that can determine
whether your produce has been mishandled, or an oven that
refuses to cook questionable meat. These are not the things of
science fiction; they are the children of the Third Wave.

All of this will take place at the convergence of demo-
graphic, lifestyle, and tech trends that will also shape the
direction of food's future. Millennials, now greater in number than baby boomers, are generally more food-centric
and more experience-centric. They tend to eat out far more
than other generations, and they also tend to be much more
health-conscious. According to the *New York Times*, per cap-
ita soda sales fell 25 percent between 1998 and 2015, replaced
mostly by water. That demand for healthier food can be seen
in the way fast casual restaurants like Sweetgreen—which
my firm, Revolution, invested in—are eating away at the
fast food market. Unlike McDonald's, Sweetgreen isn't using
tech to process foods; they're using it to manage the logistics of a seasonal farm-to-table operation. That, in turn, has
contributed to the revival of artisan farmers, who are able to
sell fresh produce at better prices than they could get selling
through distributors.

This trend isn't lost on investors. When they look at food-tech startups to fund, it will be those best able to tap into that culture—those best able to reap value from a healthy eating revolution.

SURF'S UP

When I was growing up in Hawaii, I'd often head to the beach to bodysurf. One afternoon I watched a fellow surfer riding the waves with easy confidence. He was much better than I was. I paddled over to him, waiting for another swell to come our way, and asked if he had any advice he could offer.

"There's only one thing you need to know," he said. "When the wave is cresting, you're either in the tube or you're in the sand."

The Third Wave is cresting. And whether you're an entrepreneur looking to embrace it or a corporation trying to brace for it, this is not an event you can afford to ignore.

FOUR

START UP, SPEED UP

DESPITE AOL'S success, there was always a feeling that just around the corner, there could be a new technology lurking—a fierce new competitor ready to pounce. There were a few startups popping up, and we kept our eyes on them, but most of our fears were focused on the big companies making moves in the space. Some of the world's largest and best-capitalized companies—General Electric, Microsoft, and AT&T among them—were plotting to enter the market, and we worried that if they attacked with overwhelming force, we could be squashed.

We also had to worry about Prodigy, which in the late '80s was one of the largest online services. Their initial product was a little clunky. Prodigy spent millions of dollars conducting research about what consumers might want but misread the signals, and ended up designing a flawed product. They talked to "typical" consumers via focus groups in shopping malls all across the country, and the feedback they got led them to design a service for people who had never used a PC. But their primary market, at least initially, was people who *were* using PCs, and who were getting used to graphical user interfaces like Windows. All their applications used similar menuing interfaces, and they expected their online service to do so as well.

Still, we had real concerns about the company. Prodigy had the backing of IBM, CBS, and Sears, who together put hundreds of millions of dollars into user acquisition. They were a very real threat.

We plotted and planned, then made a couple of clever moves to maintain our edge. The first was a deal we did with IBM to create a private-label online service called Promenade. At the time, no one could understand why IBM would agree to partner with us after having spent $500 million to launch a competitor. But we had found the perfect opening.

A few years earlier, IBM's first home computer, the PCjr, had failed. IBM executives didn't want it to cannibalize sales of their higher-margin business PCs, so they crippled the PCjr's capabilities, and consumers rejected it, choosing to buy from Apple and Commodore instead. IBM wanted to relaunch a home computer, and was committed to getting it right this time. So they set up a dedicated team, freed from the corporate bureaucracy, and tasked it with designing, manufacturing, and marketing a computer that would (finally) resonate with the growing consumer PC market.

The IBM team came to visit us. We were worried that they might just be visiting to gain some intelligence for Prodigy, but we decided to engage with them and try to turn things to our advantage. We urged them to be the first consumer PC manufacturer to build a modem into every PC as a standard item (up until then, it had been sold as an add-on "peripheral" device). They decided to do so, in part to help Prodigy.

Once we knew IBM was going to make modems a standard feature of their new home computers, we plotted to get our service into their bundle. After several discussions with IBM and lots of internal brainstorming, we came up with an interesting angle. We reminded IBM that Prodigy was available to every PC user, so including Prodigy in their bundle would offer no real differentiation to potential PC buyers. So, we argued, IBM should pay us to create a proprietary service. We suggested that it have a learning focus so that it would appeal to parents who were buying the computer to give their kids an edge. IBM agreed to the deal and agreed to pay us several million dollars to create the new service, called Promenade. Needless to say, Prodigy wasn't pleased.

We also figured out a cheap and easy way to go directly after Prodigy's customers. Prodigy, like other online services, was testing different ways to monetize the platform. At some point, they decided to start charging companies to send emails through their system to Prodigy subscribers. So we figured, if other companies could sell their products directly to Prodigy subscribers, why not AOL? We got in contact with a sales executive within Prodigy who agreed to let us do just that. We sent emails offering AOL to Prodigy subscribers via Prodigy's own email service. We were one of the first customers of this new marketing service and quickly became a meaningful source of revenue for them. Prodigy would spend hundreds of millions of dollars to build their membership, and we would spend a few million to cherry-pick their customers. This arrangement lasted about a year, until somebody higher up figured out that while they were generating revenue in the short run, they were doing so in the least strategic way imaginable.

Another big potential threat was CompuServe. One of the earliest online services, the company was owned by H&R Block and headquartered in Columbus, Ohio. In the early days, most would have predicted that CompuServe would emerge as the dominant player in the market. They were much larger than we were, and watched us with some concern as we started to get traction. When they concluded we were a real threat, they decided to contain the threat by trying to acquire us. They approached Jim Kimsey and initially offered $50 million. As their offer climbed to $60 million, interest in selling rose. Jim was in favor of selling, as he was worried about the coming competition, convinced that our early momentum could dissipate under the inevitable onslaught. The board was split, with about half favoring a take-the-money-and-run sale now and the other half inclined to stay the course as an independent company. I was forced to push back aggressively, advocating strongly against selling. "It is crazy to sell now," I told the board. "It's the bottom of the first inning, and this market is only now about to take off." I implored them to remember our grander ambitions, even threatening to resign in protest if the sale went through. Eventually I prevailed, defeating the acquisition by a single vote.

A lesser-known competitor was GEnie, a service from General Electric. When GEnie first came on the scene, I was very nervous. As competitors go, America's most iconic brand is not generally the one you want to go up against. They should have been our biggest threat.

As it turned out, the project wasn't a priority of the company's. It wasn't even a priority of the division it was created under. It turned out to be the pet project of a handful of employees, and it had very little attention or resources behind it. Partly for that reason, GEnie's head of marketing, Jean Wackes, applied for a job with us in 1988. She started working for us shortly thereafter and became one of our most important executives. Ten years later, we were married in a private ceremony at our home in McLean, Virginia.

THE 800-POUND GORILLA IN SEATTLE

As careful as we were in monitoring GEnie, Prodigy, and CompuServe, the true threat, in our eyes, was Microsoft.

We had already had some difficulty with Microsoft. Soon after AOL went public, in 1992 Paul Allen, one of the founders of Microsoft, started buying our stock—then quickly bought more. Initially, we were friendly about it and started having discussions with Allen and his team about ways we could work together. We told him we'd be comfortable having him buy up to 10 percent of our shares. But he kept buying. We got worried that he might be planning to launch a hostile takeover (perhaps fronting for Microsoft, as he remained a board member and large shareholder), so our board hired investment bankers, who advised us to put a "poison pill" in place to block such a move. The board decided to meet to approve such a provision, which would have allowed Allen or others to buy up to 15 percent of our stock but no more. As the board was meeting to vote on the poison pill, we learned that Allen's buying had accelerated, and that he had already passed the 15 percent threshold, essentially negating the value of the planned provision. The board had no choice but to raise the threshold to 20 percent.

The board also decided that we couldn't trust Allen. We put ourselves on a war footing, preparing for what many assumed was an inevitable hostile takeover attempt. Microsoft was plotting to enter the online market itself, and we knew that they were debating whether it would be better to build something themselves or invest in or acquire an existing online company. I flew with our team to Seattle to meet with Allen and his advisors. We told him we had passed the poison pill, limiting him to a 20 percent stake. We told him we would aggressively oppose any efforts to take over the company. And, because he had breached our trust, we would no longer consider offering him a board seat and would no longer be willing to partner with him in any capacity. It was a difficult meeting—Allen felt he should be able to do whatever he wanted (at one point he said, "This is America" and suggested that our moves were anti-American).

After a few months of our freezing him out, he realized we were serious. We encouraged him to sell his 20 percent stake and offered to help him find a buyer. I spent a few months trying to place the stake in friendly hands, including Time Warner's. Our advocate in that effort was Walter Isaacson, then head of new media for Time Inc. Walter had already been one of AOL's earliest—and most respected—partners. He was one of the digital pioneers, responsible for making *Time* one of the very first magazines to go online. He saw the potential in the Internet at a time when most people were dismissing it as a fad, and he saw enormous upside potential for Time Warner to purchase a stake in our future. But he couldn't get any support internally. Skepticism about the Internet ran deep at Time Warner—a lesson I would relearn many times.

Tensions with Microsoft continued, and soon I was returning to Seattle, this time at Bill Gates's invitation. It's hard to fully capture how dominant Microsoft was in those days, or how aggressive they would be in situations like this. This was not the first time Gates had held a meeting like this; it was part of his modus operandi. To stay on top, Microsoft had made a habit of buying potential competitors and using their market dominance to leverage a favorable deal for themselves. The message was simple: Accept our terms or we'll destroy you. It was not an empty threat.

· · ·

When I arrived in Seattle, I knew what to expect from him but wasn't sure what to expect from myself. Would he be able to tell I was nervous? Would my sweaty palms give me away? I waited for a few minutes in the lobby before being ushered into his office.

"Come on in, Steve," he said, pointing to a chair across the desk. We shook hands and then got right down to business. He started by praising AOL effusively, telling me how impressed he was with what we'd built, how well it was designed, and how much traction it was gaining. He told me that we deserved credit for creating the consumer online market and that we should be proud. Then came the squeeze.

"We think the online market is extremely significant," he said, "and I want you to know that Microsoft has every intention of being the dominant player." I tried not to react, to steel myself for what was coming next.

He told me about a competitive service Microsoft was developing, which would be called MSN. It would work much like AOL, but, he disclosed, unlike AOL, MSN would be bundled with every copy of Microsoft's Windows operating system. That meant that in almost every PC coming onto the market, MSN would be the default portal to the Internet.

"I tell you this as a courtesy, Steve," he said, the threat implicit in his words.

"But there is an alternative. We'd consider acquiring all of AOL, possibly even just a part of it. If it was up to us, we'd rather have you on our team than left out in the cold."

I told him I would take the offer back with me. And I did my best not to show my cards. But when I left his office, I was shaken. This was a threat, and I had no idea how we would overcome it.

Our board held a special meeting to discuss the Microsoft situation. As a public company, we had a fiduciary responsibility to entertain any acquisition offer seriously. There was considerable debate, as many did favor a sale, and did fear Microsoft's entry into the market. But ultimately I was able to convince the board that a sale was still premature. If Paul Allen was so eager to buy the company and now Bill Gates was, too, we must be on to something, I argued. After going back and forth on the merits of entertaining a formal offer from Microsoft, we decided to shut down any discussions. I called Gates and told him our board had met and decided we had no interest in entertaining an acquisition, as we believed we could create a lot of value for shareholders if we remained an independent company. Gates seemed surprised and a little miffed, and he reminded us that Microsoft would soon enter the market in an aggressive, win-at-all-costs way.

Not long after, we finally cut a deal to sell Allen's stake to John Malone, CEO of the cable giant TCI (Tele-Communications Inc.). But the night before the transaction was supposed to take place, Bill Gates offered Malone a 20 percent stake in MSN instead. Gates didn't want TCI in our camp, fearing that Malone would help line up the cable industry to support AOL. Malone walked away from our deal. (He later told me that it was the worst investment decision he'd ever made, as he made little on his MSN investment, and, by jilting us at the altar, he passed up the opportunity to make billions as an AOL shareholder.) Eventually, Paul Allen sold his stock back into the market. But Microsoft was clearly a threat—and they wanted us to know it.

There was a lot of tension at AOL headquarters. We increasingly felt that Microsoft could easily use its monopoly power to put our little upstart out of business. And the perception wasn't just internal. The market was similarly skittish; our stock tumbled.

We knew it was important to reassure our employees, who were understandably concerned and anxious. So we called a company meeting that looked kind of like a corporate pep rally. Ted Leonsis was one of the key speakers. He created a giant dinosaur poster, and he used it as a prop in a rousing speech— about how Microsoft was a dinosaur, and how we would prevail. At the end of the meeting, the entire staff signed the dinosaur poster. Everybody left pumped up, ready for battle.

A BULLET DODGED

In August 1995, Microsoft launched MSN in tandem with the launch of their new Windows 95 operating system. As Gates had promised—and we had feared—MSN was now a standard feature of Windows, with the MSN icon prominently displayed on the opening Windows screen. But that wasn't all. Microsoft decided to attack AOL where we were most vulnerable, which was our pricing. Our monthly subscription fee included use of some services, but hourly charges would kick in for premium services. By contrast, MSN announced that they would offer unlimited Internet access for a flat fee of $19.95 a month. We learned about that on a Friday. That night, I decreed that we had to match the MSN pricing, and that we had to work through the weekend so we could announce our new $19.95 pricing on Monday morning. Many folks on our executive team argued against the move, but I knew that we had to do it to remain competitive, and that we had to act quickly, before MSN got traction. First thing Monday morning, we announced that we were going to $19.95 unlimited as well. The strategy worked—we hobbled Microsoft at launch, while fueling further momentum for AOL.

But the move wasn't without consequences.

With unlimited pricing, usage skyrocketed, creating all sorts of system problems. We couldn't add server capacity fast enough. Customers would get knocked offline and would often get a busy signal when trying to reconnect using their dial-up modems.

At the same time, Wall Street saw our costs going up and our margins going down and panicked. Our stock declined precipitously. We rushed to New York to meet with institutional investors to try to mollify them, as many were convinced that our move was rash—and likely fatal. It took a few months to work through the operational issues and add more capacity. But there was really only one way to calm investor fears, and that was to identify new revenue sources to make up for the losses from the pricing switch.

That's when we really began to embrace advertising and ecommerce, something I was uneasy about doing. I had never been a fan of online advertising, but I knew that with an unlimited pricing model, we didn't have much choice. I remember a meeting we had to discuss our first advertisement, a Sprint ad that, by today's standards, was actually fairly small. "Isn't there a way we could do this . . . you know . . . a little bit smaller?" I asked. "So it won't be so visible?" I was nearly laughed out of the room. And it was hard to blame them for laughing. I had to accept that we were moving inexorably, along with the rest of the Internet, into an advertising space that felt more like we were selling access to consumers than providing them with a service.

Over time, the model turned a profit, and by the spring of 1996 investor worries subsided. Despite the hype, MSN never got a strong foothold in the market. And we had completely turned the tables on CompuServe. A few years earlier, they had been trying to buy us. Now we were preparing to buy them. Rupert Murdoch caught wind of the acquisition and decided to sue AOL to block the deal, saying we were already too powerful. News Corp had its own nascent online competitor, Kesmai, and Murdoch was concerned that it had no real shot against us. Christopher Holden, the chief executive of Kesmai, complained that "AOL's customer base is the only commercially viable cyberspace audience on the planet."

I liked the way that sounded.

FIVE

THE THREE P's

$\mathcal{S}$ TARTING UP and speeding up is complex, often con-
founding work, as my early AOL experience makes
clear. Elon Musk once compared starting a business to "star-
ing into the face of death."[1] Whether that sounds bleak or
exhilarating is a good litmus test for whether you've got what
it takes to start and run a successful Third Wave business. The
upside, both in terms of lives improved and value created,
couldn't be higher. Indeed, the startups of the Third Wave
will collectively shape what could be one of the most thrilling
chapters in the history of American entrepreneurship. They
will be propelled by bold, ambitious thinkers, people who
know how to navigate a set of complicated challenges strate-
gically and confidently—and who relish the chance to do so.

The superstars of the Third Wave will pursue bold visions,
but their true gift will be mastery of execution. AOL was not

alone in believing in the idea of the Internet, but we out-hustled and outexecuted our competitors. The big companies, like IBM and GE, should have prevailed, but they didn't. Their lack of agility and entrepreneurial passion and culture hobbled them.

When I talk to aspiring entrepreneurs about the Third Wave, I'm often approached by people excited about the possibility but concerned with the same basic question: What do I need to do differently if I'm going to start a Third Wave company?

I tell them that it all comes down to the three P's: partnership, policy, and perseverance.

1. PARTNERSHIP

There's an old African proverb I've come to appreciate: "If you want to go quickly, go alone. If you want to go far, go together." As simple as this advice may sound, I think it's one of the most important lessons in business. It's particularly true for the Third Wave, where the success of a company will depend largely on the partnerships its leadership can forge—sometimes even with the very organizations they are trying to disrupt.

During the Second Wave, some of the most successful companies were those that essentially optimized a niche app, figured out a way to get traction, and then drove viral adoption. They were able to follow a fairly straightforward playbook:

Focus on product. Focus on audience. Don't worry about monetization until you have millions of users.

During the Third Wave, a great product will only get you so far. You typically won't be able to build an audience by dropping your app in the App Store and waiting for users to sign up. That's because most Third Wave industries have gatekeepers. There are key decision makers in school districts who will need to approve any products that have to do with classroom learning. The same is true in healthcare, transportation, finance, education, and food.

For the most part, success will hinge on an entrepreneur's ability to form constructive, supportive partnerships with the organizations and individuals that can influence those decision makers and, eventually, with the decision makers themselves. These Third Wave companies won't have the option of going it alone.

The story of Apple's work on the iPod is illustrative. Steve Jobs saw great potential in portable MP3 players when they debuted in the 1990s. But he and his fellow executives were surprised by how poorly companies were commercializing them. "The products stank," Apple vice president Greg Joswiak told *Newsweek*. So Jobs organized a team.

"Picasso had a saying," Jobs explained, according to biographer Walter Isaacson: "'Good artists copy; great artists steal'—and we have always been shameless about stealing great ideas." The nascent MP3 player and online-music industry was no exception.

I met Jobs to discuss the music business about a year before he launched the iPod. The two of us sat in a dark corner of a quiet San Francisco sushi restaurant, hoping that nobody would recognize us so we could talk in peace. At the time he was still just envisioning the iPod, and he lit up when he talked about it. I thought it was a great idea, and I encouraged him to continue to develop it and told him I would do whatever I could to be supportive. AOL later offered to be the online music store for the iPod, but Jobs decided to create his own iTunes store instead.

Soon after, Jobs put Tony Fadell, an engineer with Apple, in charge of the iPod project and gave him three key requirements: It had to be fast, simple, and beautiful. It also had to be ready by Christmas. Fadell worked with Phil Schiller, Jony Ive, and other Apple talent—and they beat the deadline. *Newsweek* rapturously described it as a "double-crystal polymer Antarctica, a blankness that screams in brilliant colors across a crowded subway." It would launch alongside iTunes.

Yet, no matter how beautiful the product or well built the software, Apple couldn't go to market alone. They still needed to license the music content, which meant building a working partnership with the same companies that would be threatened by Apple's success.

Apple handled this dilemma in a clever and artful way. They approached the music companies and told them not to worry, that iTunes only worked with Macintosh, which at the time had a meager 2 percent market share. Apple pitched iTunes as a risk-free laboratory for the record labels, the opportunity for the industry to test a different model—a model seemingly more sustainable than endlessly litigating piracy, which had been the music industry's primary strategy to that point. In the end, the pitch worked. Had Jobs been more frank about his ambition—that is, had he admitted that he was aiming for a billion users—he likely wouldn't have gotten the licenses, and iTunes would have gone the way of Bill von Meister's ill-fated Home Music Store.

This maneuver was a tightrope walk for Apple. But it would have been even harder for any other company. When Jobs approached the music labels, he was doing so as a well-known and well-respected brand in his own right. He was coming to the table with ideas and resources and a strategy that was thoughtfully de-risked.

But if a young startup had come up with the same idea, what are the chances they would have gotten the meeting? And even if they had, what was the likelihood that record labels would sit across the table from an unknown quantity and have the confidence that any partnership was worth their while? This lack of credibility may be the single greatest challenge for Third Wave startups. It's also one that can be overcome. What it requires is more partners. Different partners. Partners who can lend credibility and provide momentum and help create a sense of inevitability.

This was a particularly acute challenge in AOL's early days as well. We had to build credibility—and create a sense of possibility—not just around our company but the emerging industry itself. We had to convince p partners, first, that the Internet'would become a core part of everyday life and, second, that even though there were a lot of big companies, little AOL was the one to bet on. But we couldn't do it alone, and we had to start small. Our first deal was with Commodore, and because we did that deal, we could do one with Tandy. And because of those two, we could do a deal with Apple. And because we had Apple, we could get IBM. And because we did deals with all of them, we had the credibility that enabled us to raise capital and gain traction in the market.

We would never have gotten funding if we had said, "We're going to create this company on our own, and we're going to market it on our own. We have no brand, we have no money, we have nothing but will." That's what our biggest competitor—Prodigy—was doing, but they had $1 billion in investment. We couldn't compete against them alone. Our only chance was to stitch together enough alliances to create a sense of possibility—and, we hoped, inevitability.

Often, forging external partnerships depends on bolstering the internal team. A brilliant developer who comes up with a new way for hospitals to track patients isn't likely to get an audience—or a fair hearing—from the medical community on her reputation alone. But that dynamic changes instantly if she shows up with her newest board member, the former CEO of the Cleveland Clinic. Now she has a foot in the door, and a serious shot at a partnership. If she manages to land the deal, she's more likely to land the next one, creating a virtuous cycle of credibility. These endorsements can attract and assuage prospective investors. And credible investors will ratchet up the founder's own credibility factor even more, opening the possibility of raising a new round with others.

Securing partnerships can be very difficult. In 2005, I put together a company called Revolution Health, with the goal of (you guessed it) revolutionizing the healthcare industry. I recruited a dream team of investors and board members, made bold statements about our plans and ambitions, and launched a full-scale effort to attract the right partnerships. We invested in a company that provided health screenings at retail stores, and one that would focus on remote concierge health services. We purchased a software company that made personal health management software and another that would help small businesses and corporations form their own healthcare plans.

Some of it ended up working. We sold one company to Towers Watson for $435 million, and another, Everyday Health, is a public company today. But much of the effort fizzled. It was partly an issue of timing: A lot of the technology being leveraged to disrupt healthcare today wasn't available to us then. But it's hard to blame the timing alone. We tried to do too much too soon and we failed to secure critical partnerships. We did come close to getting the use of the Mayo Clinic brand for convenient care clinics, and almost got Walmart to team up with us. But in the end, we couldn't get the discussions across the finish line. Both concluded that it was too early and too risky to take a leap.

Partnerships in the Third Wave are the prerequisite for success. And that can create a Catch-22—where a company needs a partnership before it can get funded, but can't secure a partnership without showing proof of concept (or, at least, proof of life). Getting over that hump will require persistence—and patience.

For anyone who has worked outside of tech, this advice may sound easy and obvious. For anyone who has worked in the business, you know how hard it can be. There is an attitude and a culture among some people in the tech world, where money equals merit, and where people are celebrated for brashness.

During the Second Wave, this swashbuckling attitude often worked to the benefit of companies, but mostly because they didn't need to build partnerships. In the Third Wave, this same attitude could be devastating to a company's prospects. In the Third Wave, disruption cannot be a mantra; it has to be a strategy. And while your product has to be great, your partnership skills may end up determining your success or failure.

We saw this with the rise of MOOCs, or massive open online courses. The original idea was that these companies were going to offer a platform for learning, where anybody could be a professor and anybody could be a student. But it didn't take long before the folks behind these companies realized that they had to pivot to an enterprise model, selling the platform to companies rather than consumers. And to be credible, they realized, they had to partner with Harvard and MIT and other top schools, bringing in credible brands to give their corporate customers comfort about the quality of the learning.

The problem was, even though companies could get to market with the core MOOC technology relatively quickly, they made a lot of noise doing so. They were unwisely public in their criticism, calling universities irrelevant and pledging to drive them out of business. Then one day they realized they needed to pivot, and the very universities they had said would soon be irrelevant became important partners. One of the leading MOOC companies, Coursera, even hired the former president of Yale to become CEO. The credibility and relationships he brought were viewed as critical to the future of Coursera.

2. POLICY

Third Wave industries are some of the most regulated in the country—and usually for good reason. We don't want businesses selling drugs that haven't been approved by the FDA, or companies selling unsafe food to our children. We don't want a startup to unleash self-driving cars onto our highways or self-flying drones into our skies unless we're sure they're safe. And whether you want to build a wind farm or a solar farm, companies can't build things in the real world with the same freedom they might in the virtual world.

It doesn't matter whether you think that's a good thing

or a bad thing. It is not going to change. There are battles over unnecessary regulations—and there should be—but the changes sought, even when meaningful, are always going to be marginal in comparison to the size of the regulatory regime.

Government will always play a role in Third Wave industries, and that means Third Wave entrepreneurs must have a fluent grasp on the policy issues they will encounter. New lending platforms require Securities and Exchange Commission (SEC) clearance. Personalized genetic testing requires approval from the Food and Drug Administration (FDA). Delivery devices can't be flown without clearance from the Federal Aviation Administration (FAA). And the list goes on and on.

Third Wave entrepreneurs will need to engage with governments. The challenge, of course, is that few founders are policy wonks, and even fewer have the time (or desire) to become regulatory experts. They'll have to hire them—or at least rely on them—from the beginning. A lot of companies won't be able to get venture funding without demonstrating a credible go-to-market strategy, including how to manage regulatory issues. No matter how good an idea, a Third Wave company that lacks a clear strategy for policy is a dangerous gamble for investors. It's not that success is impossible; but the odds make it a difficult bet.

We've watched the risk factors change as each wave evolved. In the First Wave, technology risk was the great concern—can you build it? In the Second Wave, market risk was paramount—if you build it, will the masses adopt it? In the Third

Wave, policy risk will become more important—will you be able to navigate the rules and successfully bring your product or service to market?

3. PERSEVERANCE

Perseverance is part of the story of *every* successful company. But Third Wave entrepreneurship will require a special kind. A great Third Wave idea will have dozens of obstacles to viability, not just with hardware and software but with logistics and supply chains, with partnerships and policy. And it is all too easy to see any one of those obstacles as fatal. A partnership fails. A regulator objects. The company is adrift. But during the Third Wave, things can change quickly. In 2014, when genetics-testing company 23andMe was prohibited by the FDA from selling its products, many observers believed the company was dead. But less than a year later, the company was able to get a special exemption from the FDA and restart its sales. Had they not persevered, they wouldn't have been around to relish the victory.

AOL was a decade-in-the-making "overnight success," and we had many near-death experiences before we succeeded. The same will be true of many Third Wave companies. There will be the occasional come-out-of-nowhere phenomenon, but the next generation of entrepreneurs is going to need to be prepared for a long slog. And the Third Wave will require a high degree of adaptability. Your initial product may not survive its first contact with the marketplace. Or with regulators. Or, perhaps partners you seek to align with will demand some adjustments. You'll have to keep adjusting, tweaking, pivoting.

The winners of the Third Wave will be those who chase big-impact ideas with a sense of urgency—but also methodically and diplomatically. Third Wave companies will have to find a perfect balance between two competing ideas. On the one hand, disruptive success depends in some ways on ignorance. It requires a fresh perspective and the ability to look at new paradigms without being burdened by legacy dogma. The founders of PayPal like to say that if any of them had actually worked in the credit card industry, they would have been too fearful to give their new business a try. In this sense, thinking like an incumbent is a disadvantage. Yet on the other hand, understanding the dynamics at play in the industry and having a clear view of potential partnerships and policy issues will increasingly be prerequisites for success—or at least for avoiding major roadblocks. Third Wave entrepreneurs must find a way, then, to bring both viewpoints to bear—the nuanced perspective of the defending incumbent and the relentlessly disruptive mind-set of an entrepreneur on the attack.

SIX

PARDON THE DISRUPTION

A s THE Third Wave approaches, many long-established, stable, profitable corporations will be in jeopardy. A 2015 report from Reuters noted that "the top executive of many a corporate giant must feel like the fictional character Gulliver, waking up to find themselves under attack from modern-day Lilliputians, small start-up companies which overwhelm their established rivals with new technologies." Many of these industries were somewhat immune to technological changes in the first two waves of the Internet and may, as a result, face this next wave with complacency. They do so at their own peril.

Plenty of companies will sit on the sidelines, assuming all will continue to be fine. They follow a long line of businesses, once heralded, that failed to adapt and then failed to survive. Perhaps that's why business leaders said, in a 2015 survey by the Global Center for Digital Business Transformation, that nearly half of the top-ranked companies in their industries will be gone by 2020. But the Third Wave is not just a fait accompli that corporations must defend against; the best leadership teams will recognize it's something they can take advantage of. As Peter Diamandis, founder of the XPRIZE nonprofit, put it, "It isn't that entrepreneurs are smarter than companies, it's that they are trying more crazy ideas, taking more shots on goal." There will be some corporate leaders who will develop a strategy to take more shots on goal—to get in front of these opportunities rather than chasing them from behind.

The conventional wisdom may be that startups are the future, while established corporations are all relics of another world. But many of the world's biggest companies are teeming with talent and resources, creating new and innovative products all the time. In 2014, for example, Johnson & Johnson spent more than Google on research and development. And though the most rapid growth in R&D is happening in the software and Internet industry, as of 2014, less than 10 percent of total corporate R&D came from tech companies. Most of the world's biggest ideas are still hatching elsewhere.

Consider the self-driving car, a technology that has captured the imaginations of executives at Google and Uber, who are competing to develop a street-legal vehicle that will help us redefine our commutes. But the idea of a self-driving vehicle was not first born in the tech sector; it was born in the agricultural sector. Plenty of farmers were operating self-driving tractor technology before Google ever entered the space. Illinois-based John Deere was developing GPS navigation systems for its tractors more than twenty years ago—before Google was even founded.

John Deere executives may not have appreciated what they had, and they were likely not in a position to build a commercial self-driving car division from scratch. But what if they had created a spin-off company to commercialize their self-driving technology, or licensed the technology to a partner? Perhaps John Deere, a nearly two-hundred-year-old company, could have become one of the leaders in Third Wave transportation.

In some industries, the most successful Third Wave companies may also end up being the most established. They'll be the companies that took the Third Wave seriously enough to get ahead of it. But what does that entail, exactly?

MANAGING THE COMING WAVE

It starts with developing a point of view—a hypothesis that the world is changing. Just the simple act of a CEO embracing and articulating such a world view is critical. It's a way of delegating a mix of paranoia and curiosity, making people a little nervous and getting them out of their comfort zones. It's also a way of expressing optimism, rather than dread, about the future—which naturally gets employees to pay more regular, focused attention to what is happening around the edges of your industry, with an eye toward what may happen next. It's about lifting up the people in your company who are seeing around corners, and giving them the support—both emotional and financial—to innovate.

Incumbents often fail because they underestimate the speed at which the future is approaching. People at startups think about the future every day. Venture-scale investors are seeking companies with the potential to reach at least $100 million in revenue and go public. In the startup world, staggering sums of money are chasing some of the world's biggest ideas. It's only a matter of time before the right entrepreneur with the right idea connects with the right venture firm. The corporate mind-set is often to avoid mistakes, but in a world that changes rapidly, doing nothing can be the biggest mistake. Sometimes waiting for all of the facts can be riskier than taking a leap of faith.

Incumbents also fail because of the size of their organizations themselves. Frequently, large companies have a decision-making process where many people have the power to stop an idea, but very few have the authority to green-light one. This creates an environment where there is a strong bias toward "no."

Objects in the mirror are closer—far closer—than they appear. One of the biggest mistakes companies make is overlooking the impact of nascent technology. Too often corporate executives are too shortsighted to understand how technology that is disrupting a different industry might be adapted to do the same to their own. Uber might be disrupting taxi services today, for example, but as they move into the delivery business, will Uber disrupt FedEx or UPS tomorrow?

Second, corporate recruiters need to be working overtime hiring and retaining and celebrating and protecting the innovators within their walls. There is a mythology in the tech world that the best talent gravitates toward startups. But many of the smartest, most creative people in the world can be found working at some of its biggest, oldest companies. Siemens employs 90,000 research scientists. Monsanto employs some of the sharpest agriculture technology minds on the planet. GE's research labs are filled with brilliant PhDs. The raw talent is there; the question is how it is organized and whether it can be mobilized to innovate. It's not enough to employ these kinds of thinkers. They need to have a voice, along with the resources and protections that will enable them to commercialize their ideas. They need a level playing field to stay in front of their startup competitors.

The challenge for Fortune 500 CEOs is to leverage scale advantages, while injecting a tempo of speed and a culture of risk. At Facebook, engineers are encouraged to "move fast and break things," not because Mark Zuckerberg is reckless, but because he understands that innovators need the space in which to take risks. At most large companies, innovators are often discouraged from even sharing their ideas. That's self-destructive—and self-reinforcing—behavior.

EMBRACE SELF-DISRUPTION

What these transitions will ultimately require is companies willing to self-disrupt. As Steve Jobs once put it, "If you don't cannibalize yourself, someone else will." Yet the challenges of doing so are substantial for entrenched companies, and have been made famous by Harvard professor Clay Christensen in his book *The Innovator's Dilemma*. As he writes, the greatest challenge for successful companies is focusing on customers' current preferences while preparing for their future preferences. In a CBS interview, Jeff Bezos said it plainly: "Amazon will be disrupted one day. I don't worry because I know it's inevitable."

Some companies have proven successful at self-disruption. Apple's unprecedented growth has required the destruction of some of its most profitable products. The iPhone hurt iPod sales. The iPad cannibalized the MacBook. Amazon, too, has moved swiftly in this way. Having built its reputation and revenue on selling printed books, Amazon recognized that the ebook industry would rule the future. So they built it themselves—the hardware and software—and now they own the past and the future.

Of course, even when there is a desire to challenge the status quo, CEOs are often penalized for leaning too far into the future—making too many investments or taking too many risks. At PepsiCo, CEO Indra Nooyi pushed a diversification strategy, recognizing that a shift in food preferences could have bad long-term consequences for a company known for selling sugary drinks and high-calorie snacks. But doing so caused a revolt among some shareholders, who were convinced that Nooyi's attempt at transformation was hurting the stock price in the present. Where Nooyi survived, DuPont CEO Ellen Kullman did not. Just a day after Bloomberg Markets named her one of the most influential people in business, Kullman was forced out after a long battle with an activist shareholder who was frustrated that, among other things, the company was investing $2 billion a year in R&D.

The same kind of problem plagued Kodak. The conventional wisdom is that Kodak didn't see digital coming. That's just not true. In fact, the first digital camera was actually invented at Kodak in 1975 by Steven Sasson. The company was doing a lot of things right early, including a partnership with AOL. They knew that digital presented a threat to their core business in the long run, but executives were more concerned about the short run. According to *New York Times* reporter James Estrin, when Kodak executives asked when digital could compete with film, Sasson told them it could take twenty years. "When you're talking to a bunch of corporate guys about 18 to 20 years in the future, when none of those guys will still be in the company, they don't get too excited about it," Sasson told Estrin. Sadly, Kodak filed for bankruptcy in 2012.

PLAY OFFENSE

Big companies have more power than they think. They have scale, they have partners, they understand policy, and often they have global reach. These are all highly valuable assets in the Third Wave (much more so than in the Second), and they will give the world's biggest corporations the chance to play offense with confidence. Take a lesson from the Wayne Gretzky playbook; he was a great hockey player because he didn't focus on where the puck was, but where it was going.

IF YOU CAN'T BUILD THE FUTURE, INVEST IN IT

Finally, companies would be better positioned if they figured out how to better engage with entrepreneurs so that they can invest in them and own a piece of the action. Some legacy companies have developed internal venture funds, in part to have an early-warning radar system for emerging ideas, some of which may end up leading to profitable partnerships. Others have created a "SWAT" team of people whose only job is to be a connector with startups, serving as a concierge of sorts to help build bridges between executives and entrepreneurs. It's a way of making sure that clever entrepreneurial ideas find their way to the right person in the company—and that the company has a chance to invest in a future it cannot build on its own.

Ultimately, major corporations should see the Third Wave as both an extraordinary opportunity and an existential threat.

The most successful executives will embrace it with speed and agility. They will break down silos within their company, drive collaboration across divisions, and look beyond their industry for partnerships. And it is from there that they will have the perfect view of once vaunted competitors collapsing under the disruptive forces of Third Wave entrepreneurship.

SEVEN

THE RISE OF THE REST

IMAGINE IT'S a beautiful afternoon in late May in Palo Alto. The class of 2040 has just graduated from Stanford University.

Meet Jessica. She's a second-generation American. She majored in public policy and, like a majority of her classmates, computer science. She's at the top of her class. Jessica can have any job she wants—and she's gotten several offers from some of the most innovative Third Wave companies in the world.

And so after she's dropped off her cap and gown, she packs up her self-driving electric car, gets in, and tells her onboard personal assistant where she's heading. As the car drives off campus, she starts binge-watching that classic show *Silicon Valley* that she's heard so much about from her parents. It's playing on her windshield as the car merges onto the highway.

But Jessica isn't going to San Francisco. She's headed to New Orleans. And none of her peers are surprised.

By the time Jessica and her classmates are graduating from college, a quarter century from now, the entrepreneurial landscape of America will look much different than it does today.

Since the First Wave of the Internet, venture capital money in the United States has been geographically concentrated. In 2014, three-quarters of all venture dollars flowed to just three states: California, New York, and Massachusetts. Our most entrepreneurial graduates tend to head to those states, too. They go to follow the money, while the money comes to follow them. Over time this arrangement has perpetuated a virtuous cycle—a financial ecosystem—in which the best innovators and the best investors congregate in just a few places to commercialize the best ideas.

There is nothing wrong with this system. On the contrary, it is the formation of these innovation clusters, and the ecosystems of collaboration that have risen around them, that has helped advance technology. We don't want this progress to stop. At the same time, because the tech sector has been concentrated in so few areas, most of the economic gains are concentrated, too. It's what turned the Santa Clara Valley into one of the wealthiest area codes in the world. It's what produced a vast medical and biotech corridor in Massachusetts, and the jobs and tax revenue that come with it.

Yet, largely because of this concentration, the economic benefits of the growth of the technology companies have not accrued to many places in the United States. Though consumers in Ohio are just as likely to use smartphones as their counterparts in New York, far fewer are likely to be responsible for the software itself. For most of the First and Second Waves, if an engineer in Nashville wanted to start her own digital company, the only real choice was to move—either to one coast or the other.

This dynamic has caused a brain drain of sorts in the United States. Entrepreneurs are cultivating the skills and creativity to come up with great ideas in the middle of the country. But then they are taking their ideas—the company behind it, the jobs that come with it, and the economic activity that surrounds it—and moving out of town.

STARTUP NATION

But as we enter the Third Wave, this arrangement will change. In fact, it's already starting. In Durham, North Carolina, for example, seven companies at the American Tobacco Campus's tech hub had exits totaling $1.5 billion between 2013 and 2015.[1] Jessica's journey to New Orleans might be hypothetical, but this future is not. And it's an illustration of what I've referred to as "the rise of the rest." Journalist Fareed Zakaria coined that phrase to describe the rise of new economies in places like China and India. The same phenomenon is happening within the United States, as regions throughout the country begin to rise.

. . .

Over the next two decades we will see cities that were once marginalized become entrepreneurial powerhouses. We'll see dozens of startups born in places such as Denver and Kansas City and Austin and Pittsburgh. We'll see venture firms opening offices in Indianapolis and Minneapolis and Salt Lake City.

We'll hear stories from places like Buffalo, where a once abandoned area of buildings has become the center of a new tech renaissance. As a reporter for *USA Today* wrote, "As the city slowly emerged from its funk through growth in advanced manufacturing and medical research about 15 years ago, tech and other industries began to land here this year. Today, construction cranes scatter the skyline. Construction is under way for a 1-million-square-foot SolarCity manufacturing center (valued at $1 billion), the addition of 500 IBM jobs and an extension to the University at Buffalo's medical research facilities." I've invested in two young Buffalo startups myself: Energy Intelligence, which builds technology that harvests energy from motor traffic, and POP Biotechnologies, which uses nanomedicine to develop cancer treatments.

This geographic diversity is vital to our future. According to the Kauffman Foundation, "New businesses account for nearly all net new job creation," and "new companies less than one year old have created an average of 1.5 million jobs per year over the past three decades."[2] In other words, startups are the engine of our economy. The communities they form, the talent they recruit, the products they make, the jobs they create, and the lives they improve can all be leveraged to transform communities.

For me, the rise of the rest is personal. My family goes back more than one hundred years on the Hawaiian Islands. My grandfather on my mother's side ran the general store in the town of Hilo. My other grandfather was the treasurer of a sugar plantation on the island of Kauai. Both of my parents went to college (and my dad got a law degree) on the mainland, but then went straight back to Hawaii. But when it was my turn to leave for school on the mainland, I did so knowing I would likely never go back. It wasn't that I had negative feelings about Hawaii. It was home—and in many ways still is. But I knew I wanted to paint on a bigger canvas, and that reaching for such ambitions wouldn't be possible from Honolulu. So there's something personally exciting about knowing that this will soon change for the next generation of entrepreneurs, whether they live in Honolulu or Houston.

I also see the rise of the rest as an investment strategy. Some of the best ideas in the world are being hatched in cities that too few venture capitalists pay attention to. For the past several years, I've been getting out of my office, and onto a bus, to see what's going on in the rest of the country. I've traveled to two dozen cities across as many states and seen communities and accelerators thriving in unlikely places. I've listened to pitches from companies few have ever heard of, with ideas I wish I'd had myself. I found Artiphon in Nashville, the maker of a tech-enabled musical instrument that went on to raise the most money in history for its category on Kickstarter and was named one of *Time* magazine's 25 Best Inventions of 2015. I found Shinola in Detroit. Founder Tom Kartsotis believed Detroit would be a comeback city, and he decided to grow Shinola in a Detroit building that once housed automobile innovation. Hundreds of former autoworkers have been retrained to craft beautiful watches, bicycles, handbags, and notebooks. And Shinola's "Where American is Made" ethos is being brought to cities around the world, including New York, London, and Washington, DC. We wrote Shinola the largest check in my investment firm's history. In fact, we're on track to invest more than $1 billion in rise-of-the-rest cities, and that's just the beginning.

THE THIRD WAVE AND THE RISE

There are three main reasons I'm confident that major new innovation centers will emerge and flourish around the country. Among them, the most significant is the Third Wave. The rise of the rest and the Third Wave are two different phenomena. But they are colliding—and converging—in self-reinforcing ways.

Most of the industries that are targets for Third Wave entrepreneurs are already clustered throughout the country. And so for many Third Wave entrepreneurs, there is appeal to putting down roots where industry ecosystems already exist. During the Second Wave, the industry of focus was technology, and so Second Wave entrepreneurs understandably flocked to the place in the country where tech companies and investors had clustered. But during the Third Wave, though products will be tech-enabled, they won't be tech-centric. They'll use apps, but the product won't be an app. And so the benefit derived from being surrounded by the tech world won't be as high. Instead, being surrounded by experts in the industry you're trying to disrupt may reap the biggest dividends.

It may make sense, for example, for a company that wants to revolutionize the agricultural industry to settle in the Midwest, where the right supply chains already exist and the culture of farmers is best understood. A company that wants to disrupt the healthcare industry might find that doing it in Nashville or Baltimore, both of which have developed vibrant healthcare sectors, might make more sense than doing it from Palo Alto or New York City. And entrepreneurs pushing the limits of robotics technology may find a welcome home in Pittsburgh, the steel city and manufacturing powerhouse where Carnegie Mellon, a research university with arguably the world's best robotics program, is located. Of course, many will still head to Silicon Valley, but less so than we've experienced in the past. Ultimately, entrepreneurs will want to be in the place where the highest concentration of related expertise is to be found.

coming years, I expect to see lots of tech entre-
id engineers who started in the Bay Area consider
relocating in search of industry-specific expertise. And the
Third Wave explosion of new kinds of startups won't just be
driven by these entrepreneurial carpetbaggers. We'll also see
industry veterans and local innovators start companies in the
rise-of-the-rest regions where they already live, to solve the
problems they know and understand.

The Second Wave had many inspiring stories of twenty-
something computer coders creating multibillion-dollar companies. The Third Wave will have similar stories, but the
founders are less likely to be twenty-something coders and
more likely to be thirty-something farmers and factory workers and chefs and artists—people who saw a problem in their
own spheres of expertise, then leveraged the skills of others to
build great companies.

That was certainly true for Jewel Burks, the founder of
Partpic and the winner of our rise-of-the-rest pitch competition in Atlanta. These competitions pit local entrepreneurs
against one another for a $100,000 investment prize. Jewel
was working in Atlanta for an industrial parts company and
noticed that she was frequently receiving calls from upset
customers who had mistakenly received the wrong part. Jewel
realized that while these customers were looking for specific
parts—a bolt for this, a rivet for that—a lot of people didn't
know the actual name or number of the part. So there was

a lot of guesswork, and a lot of frustration when customers didn't get what they needed.

Jewel had an idea. She called her friend Jason Crain, who worked at the music recognition company Shazam. Jewel and Jason came up with a concept for a product that would recognize parts not by description but by sight. Just snap a picture of the part you needed to replace, and the software would identify what the part was and send it on its way to you.

This kind of real-world solution might lead to a valuable Third Wave company, but it's an idea few people with traditional startup backgrounds would ever have pursued. They wouldn't have had the experience taking those phone calls, or understood the prevalence of the problem, or the scale of the opportunity.

Of course, while the Third Wave will play a big role in the rise of the rest, it is not the only factor driving it. There's also a cultural element. Sure, California is a terrific place to live and work, but not everyone who goes out there wants to stay forever. If you're a midwesterner, the opportunity to work for a startup in the state where you grew up could be a major selling point, the chance both to be in a place that fits your lifestyle and to give back to a community whose future you already have a stake in.

And there are related financial considerations, too. The rise-of-the-rest cities I've been visiting have a much lower cost of living. San Francisco is one of the most expensive cities in the world. So is New York. If you start a company in a city like Cincinnati, where the cost of living is lower, the overhead costs for your company will drop. A $100,000 seed investment might be enough of a spark to get a venture-scale business growing rapidly in Cincinnati. In San Francisco, that same $100,000 might only be enough to hire a part-time engineer and rent a few cubicles in a shared office space.

OPPORTUNITY IN THE BIG EASY

The playwright Tennessee Williams is sometimes quoted as having said, "America only has three cities: New York, San Francisco and New Orleans. Everywhere else is Cleveland." And while I might disagree with that second part, the first was, at one point, a pretty accurate description.

New Orleans has long been a major economic hub. Before there were major railways or airplane runways, there was just the Mississippi River, carrying people and goods in and out of the city. In 1840, the city was "rated . . . as the fourth port in point of commerce in the world, exceeded only by London, Liverpool, and New York."[3] But more recently, it was battered, and nearly broken, by the tragedy of Hurricane Katrina.

In August 2005, Hurricane Katrina swept through New Orleans and the surrounding areas with winds topping 125 miles per hour.[4] We all watched with horror as the levees failed and the streets flooded. At one point, 80 percent of the city was submerged.[5] Nearly two thousand people lost their lives. New Orleans emerged a shell of what it once was.

Even before the storm, New Orleans public schools were struggling. Only 30 percent of students were enrolled in passing schools. Graduation rates and test scores were depressingly low.

Jen Medbery came to New Orleans in 2008, less than three years after Katrina struck, to teach math as one of the founding faculty members of a new charter school. Jen already knew her way around a classroom. She had just spent two years doing Teach for America in rural Arkansas, and before that, she had earned her computer science degree at Columbia University.

While teaching, Jen noticed that she and her colleagues were spending far too much time recording data by hand—absences, grades, detentions—or by cobbling it together in complicated spreadsheets. Though they collected the data, they were not spending much time analyzing it, sharing it with one another, or using it to make better decisions. Doing that would take time and energy, precious resources needed for students in the classroom.

In 2009, Jen founded Kickboard, a company that makes it easier for schools to understand, and benefit from, the data they collect. The platform helps teachers look at their classes as a whole, and track their students across classes, to examine the big picture. If a student in my class is also doing poorly in your class, we should probably talk. If that same student happens to be doing well in a third class, or on writing assignments but not quizzes, her teacher might be able to figure out why.

And it's not just about helping teachers. Principals can now see how their individual teachers are performing, and tailor professional development and other administrative decisions around school-wide data. If several teachers are having the same classroom management issue, what new discipline policy can be put in place? If a specific reading standard isn't being met, what resources can we allocate to the reading teachers?

At the same time, parents are able to track their students' performance in real time. If Billy has gotten his second detention this week, or Maria has uncharacteristically missed a homework assignment, parents can be clued in and communicate with teachers. Because of the emphasis on data, if Jamie has failed a quiz, parents can understand if this failure was a fluke or a sign of a larger problem, and work with teachers on how best to intervene.

New Orleans was the perfect testing ground for Kickboard because, post-Katrina, nearly every public school in the city became a charter school. The relative independence of charter schools, and the startup nature of the rebuilt school system, allows them to adopt new school-wide practices quickly. As a result, charter schools in New Orleans began embracing Kickboard—and other companies like it—with interest and excitement. As Jen told the *Times-Picayune*, "There is no other city in the country that allows for that amount of innovation."[6]

New Orleans is now making a name for itself as a place where education technology companies can build partnerships and innovate in ways nearly impossible anywhere else. If this relationship continues, there is an inevitability to the success it will breed. Already there are organizations like Tim Williamson's Idea Village that are building a movement around supporting local entrepreneurs like Jen. Inevitably, this environment will drive more education pioneers to come to New Orleans—to join Teach for America or startups. More edtech, or education technology, companies will be born in New Orleans. Then investors interested in edtech will follow, funding a new generation of technology and creating a self-sustaining ecosystem. This is well under way. By 2012, New Orleans already had one startup for every 200 people—a number 56 percent higher than the national average. What once seemed impossible now seems inevitable: New Orleans, a city many were tempted to give up on, is rising again.

LOWERING BARRIERS

The rise of the rest matters. Combined with the Third Wave, it has the power to reshape the identity of dozens of cities around the country. And it means that the transformative economic value of the Third Wave can be widely shared.

The moment's significance, though, is not confined to economics. The rise of the rest will also bring diversity—both of people and ideas—which is something our country needs.

Silicon Valley has a well-documented diversity problem. According to the *New York Times,* Facebook reported that only 4 percent of its employees in the United States were Hispanic in 2015, while only 2 percent were black. At Google, the numbers are similar, and have been for years.[7]

The rise of the rest can mean diversity of opportunity. It can mean breaking the cycle of money flowing to the same kinds of people for the same kinds of ideas. It can mean the growth of businesses focused on fixing the problems in America's backyard, not just in San Francisco's. And it can mean lowering the barrier to entry across the board for entrepreneurs, no matter their background or geography.

The rise of the rest isn't just going to spread the rewards of the Third Wave around; it's going to create more of them. We will see more people starting more companies to solve more problems and seize more opportunities—many of which will never land on Silicon Valley's radar. And I believe the leaders behind these emerging companies will end up being the most diverse group of CEOs America has ever produced.

THE CHALLENGES

I do want to be clear, though. For all the potential benefits that come with building a company outside of the three big hubs, there are also plenty of challenges that companies will need to overcome, most of which are not easily remedied with a plane ticket or a moving van.

Part of being a company coming from outside Silicon Valley is dealing with the perception that, as an outsider, what you're doing must not be valuable.

I was in London recently at a conference for entrepreneurs and investors and quizzed people about the difference in valuations between London-based companies and those located in Silicon Valley. The general sense was that valuations in London were sometimes as little as half the valuations in San Francisco. London is a global metropolis and financial center, and it has a hot startup scene. But the reality is, it is largely ignored by most venture investors. Can you imagine what that valuation gap might be if you were building a startup in Des Moines?

And that kind of gap is not just a blow to your self-esteem or your hometown pride. Having that lower valuation means that you're also likely to have a lot less access to capital. And without it, the practical benefit of locating somewhere with a lower overhead might not end up mattering as much as you had hoped.

And yet, in the long run, the valuations of rise-of-the-rest startups will normalize. Early funding rounds may come with a valuation discount. But once a company has a proven track record of growth, the private markets will take notice. When Amazon acquired Zappos in Las Vegas, or Salesforce acquired ExactTarget in Indianapolis, they paid full price. There was no discount because of the location.

There are also real challenges when it comes to talent. How do you convince an engineer living in Brooklyn that she should move to Boise? It won't always be easy.

But I've also seen the flip side to these challenges. In the 1950s, Silicon Valley was just an apple orchard until William Shockley decided to start his semiconductor company there. Likewise, the Washington, DC, region was predominantly the land of government contractors until entrepreneurs like Bill von Meister decided to build a startup there. That's how CVC—and later AOL—came to be located nearly three thousand miles from Silicon Valley, in the suburbs of Washington.

It was hard in the beginning. We were raising money from New York, San Francisco, Chicago, Boston—even Toronto—but not from anyone in Washington. And we were trying to convince people to leave stable jobs in DC to join a struggling startup—a much harder sell in a city whose culture doesn't generally reward risk. At the same time, the people we did hire were self-selecting to be part of our company, which meant they probably believed in our mission more than someone in the Bay Area who jumps from startup to startup. That helped us build a stronger culture and a stronger team.

It was also easier to attract people with government experience to our team than it might have been had we been based in California. Al Haig, President Ronald Reagan's secretary of state, joined our board in the mid-1980s, which gave us a lot of credibility and a lot of useful insights. Frank Raines joined our board in the late 1990s, shortly after he stepped aside as head of the White House Office of Management and Budget. Colin Powell also joined our board at that time. Much to my delight, Colin was one of the most active users of our beta products and a quick critic when our design was flawed. We also hired a number of executives after they left government jobs. We had a home court advantage, too, able to spend more time, build more relationships, and have more influence with some of the most powerful people in the country.

Thirty years ago, Washington, DC, was much like emerging rise-of-the-rest cities today. And having watched DC grow into a major startup hub has given me confidence as I see the same pattern replicating itself across the country.

When the Smithsonian's American History Museum recently put together an exhibit called Places of Invention, Silicon Valley, not surprisingly, made the list. But what about Hartford, Connecticut? Or Medical Alley, Minnesota? Or Fort Collins, Colorado? They made the list, too.[8]

Throughout our history, innovation has come out of unlikely places. And it will again: Magic Leap, a virtual reality company in stealth mode, has already raised over $1 billion from investors including Google and Alibaba. Guess where they are located? Fort Lauderdale, Florida. This likely would not have been possible in the Second Wave, when cutting-edge tech companies were expected to be in Palo Alto (leveraging Stanford PhDs) or Boston (packed with MIT graduates).

The rise of the rest is beginning to happen, and the momentum will continue to build over the next decade.

EIGHT

IMPACT INVESTING

FOR DECADES, Milton Friedman's old maxim—"the social responsibility of business is to increase its profits"— has been the equivalent of religious doctrine, particularly among investors. CEOs who view their role as having dual purposes—a focus on both profits and social impact—are often the targets of angry investors, who see any money diverted from the margin as unrealized return. But this posture is starting to change, at a pace that could make what's become known as "impact investing" a megatrend in the Third Wave.

One hundred years ago, the focus of most investors was largely on return. But over time, and after events like the Great Depression, there was a recognition that investors also needed to factor in risk. Today, the element of impact is being injected into the investment approach as well. Impact investing is a bridge between traditional business and philanthropy—and between financial return and social good. When someone invests in a new company, the hope is that he'll eventually make that money back, and then some. When someone contributes to a nonprofit, on the other hand, there won't be any financial return, only the expectation that something good will come from it. Impact investing provides the best of both worlds. You can generate a financial return while enabling a societal benefit—driving both profit and purpose.

THE RISE OF IMPACT INVESTING

The Third Wave and impact investing are not the same phenomenon, but, like the rise of the rest, they are happening at the same time and reinforcing each other. In fact, the emergence of the Third Wave is one of several reasons why impact investing will continue its transformation from an idea on the margins to a genuine global trend.

Indeed, because of the impact Third Wave industries have on our lives, the most successful startups will already consider social benefit as a core tenet of their missions. That commitment to impact will make them attractive to those who are seeking to reshape the world with their investments. And the influx of "impact" investments will only further encourage other companies to adopt a similar model.

Much like the Third Wave, impact investing is being driven largely by the preferences of the millennial generation. As investors, millennials, when compared with other age segments, are far more committed to creating positive social change with their investment decisions. As employees, members of this generation, which is the fastest-growing part of the workforce, report actively choosing jobs because of the impact of the company they work for, and see investments as a way to demonstrate their values. And as customers, millennials want to make a positive impact with their purchases. Increasingly, in order to attract the very best people, keep customer loyalty, and bring in investment, companies are going to have to do well and do good at the same time.

Impact investing has also been encouraged by policymakers. In June 2013, the governments of the G8 created the Social Impact Investment Taskforce to help develop an impact-focused marketplace. In the U.S., dozens of states have passed laws creating a new governance option for such companies, known as benefit corporations, or B corporations. A benefit corporation builds purpose and impact into its corporate charters so its executives and boards are able to manage based on a series of metrics—such as job creation or environmental impact—and not focus exclusively on maximizing profits. By 2015, there were more than 1,500 of these B corporations, including Kickstarter, Warby Parker, Patagonia, and Etsy.

Perhaps most importantly, impact investing is on the rise because it's been proven to work. Most investors still subscribe to the Milton Friedman view that companies should focus solely on profits. These critics of impact investing worry that trying to manage with an eye on purpose as well as profits will create confusing incentives and will result in suboptimal financial performance. In the words of one skeptic, impact investing is kind of like a houseboat: It's not a good house, and it's not a good boat.

But the facts say something different. The Wharton School released a report in 2015 that evaluated fifty-three private equity funds and found that impact funds were able to achieve targeted returns and successful, mission-aligned exits. The report is encouraging and suggests that impact investing is less like a houseboat and more like brunch, as I once heard it described: better than breakfast, and better than lunch.

THE CASE FOUNDATION STORY

My wife, Jean, and I are longtime believers in the maxim that to whom much is given, much is expected. As part of our effort to live by those words, Jean left AOL in 1996 to start and run The Case Foundation, which we founded together in 1997.

At first, we assumed we had to follow a specific formula: quietly writing checks to important causes. We didn't even have a website, preferring a more below-the-radar approach. The irony—that the foundation made possible by the Internet didn't use the Internet—wasn't lost on any of us. We funded dozens of organizations such as Special Olympics and Habitat for Humanity, and we're proud of the impact our dollars had. We also launched a handful of our own initiatives, such as PowerUP, to bridge the digital divide.

But over time, we started having a different kind of conversation with organizations. They told us that, while they appreciated the money, our real value wasn't in the checks we were writing but in the visibility and credibility we were providing. It was the people and networks we could connect people to that mattered. Over time, we realized that we could have a greater impact if we focused less on what we earned in the private sector and more on what we learned from our experience. We started leveraging the skills that had made us successful— building coalitions around causes we cared about; developing partnerships across sectors, among companies, nonprofits, and government. It sparked a different way of giving back.

Impact investing was a natural fit. As traditional funding streams for social impact began to come under pressure, Jean started making the case that we needed "all oars in the water." She argued that the only way to attack social challenges was to do it together—business, government, philanthropy, and nonprofits working in tandem. We made a commitment to accelerate the growth of impact investing, and we've been working on it ever since.

Sometimes our impact investing has been financial in nature. We've invested in impact funds that are working on everything from the diagnosis and treatment of brain diseases to creating startup opportunities in the Palestinian technology sector. But most of our work has been about fostering partnerships. When the White House wanted to launch an initiative called Startup America, aimed at accelerating regional

I was born and raised in Honolulu, Hawaii. On my first birthday, Hawaii became the 50th state.

My family in Honolulu in 1967: from left, me, my older brother Danny, my father Dan, my mother Carol, my older sister Carin, and my younger brother Jeff.

When I was attending Williams College in the late 1970s I was the lead singer in a band—but I didn't sing very well. I decided to switch to the business side.

My first TV interview, on PBS's *Computer Chronicles* in 1986. I was 28 years old at the time—and really nervous.

STEVE CASE
V.P. Marketing
QUANTUMLINK

Our first brand, QuantumLink, launched in 1985 as "the online service that's easy-to-use, inexpensive, useful and fun." At the time just 3% of Americans were online, for—on average—only one hour per week.

At what became AOL, our Friday beer blasts were a good way to get a sense of what was on our team's mind. Here I am with co-founder (and CTO) Marc Seriff, early employee Keith Barron, and co-founder (and founding CEO) Jim Kimsey in 1989.

America Online screen, circa 1999. At its peak, AOL handled nearly half of all consumer Internet traffic in the U.S. It was "the Internet and a whole lot more" for most Americans. AOL was, for its time, Google, Facebook, Twitter, Amazon, Spotify, YouTube, and Instagram combined.

On Wall Street the day AOL was listed on the New York Stock Exchange. AOL was the first Internet company to go public, raising $11 million at a $70 million valuation in 1992. Eight years later, AOL was worth $160 billion, making it the best performing stock of the decade.

Those AOL disks became an American icon. We distributed hundreds of millions of them in the 1990s to encourage people to try our service. It worked: we grew from 200,000 customers in 1992 to 25 million a decade later.

The first of many magazine covers: AOL was going from being unknown and irrelevant, to central and much talked about. I used to joke that AOL was a "10 years in the making overnight success."

Discussing the constructive role that the Internet could play around protecting children with then-First Lady Hillary Clinton at the White House Conference on Children, Violence & Responsibility in 1999.

David Hume Kennerly

AP Photo

With President Clinton watching a student get online in February 2000. What we all now take for granted was big news back then. The Case Foundation's PowerUP initiative built 1,000 computer centers in underserved communities to help bridge the digital divide.

Luke Frazza

Meeting with President George W. Bush and Disney CEO Michael Eisner at the White House. When he was campaigning in 2000, I failed to convince Bush to adopt "open access" for broadband, and that contributed to our decision to later merge with Time Warner. We also considered a merger with Disney, but that idea didn't go far.

After years of battling, AOL and Microsoft announced a truce in 1996. Bill Gates agreed to bundle AOL software with Windows, in exchange for AOL integrating Microsoft's web browser.

I met Rev. Billy Graham at the TED conference in 1998. We became close friends, and traveled together on many occasions. When Jean and I were married, Graham officiated. Here we are together at the 2000 Ronald Reagan Freedom Award Dinner.

Fortune magazine hosted a global CEO forum in China in 1999, on the occasion of the 50th anniversary of the creation of the People's Republic of China. Time Warner CEO Jerry Levin chatted with me and my wife Jean at a chilly Beijing event. The seed for the AOL Time Warner merger was planted that week.

Celebrating the announcement of the merger of AOL and Time Warner in 2000 with Jerry Levin and Ted Turner. We were all smiles that day.

The "victory" shot that I later came to regret. I had agreed to step aside as CEO to enable the merger between AOL and Time Warner to occur. But on the day of the announcement, I wanted to look upbeat. I later regretted this, because it led to the perception I was running AOL Time Warner, not just chairing the board.

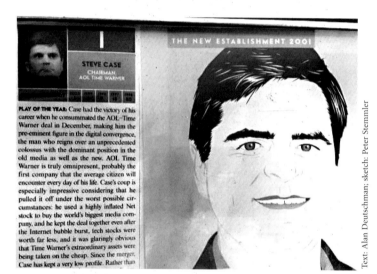

THE NEW ESTABLISHMENT 2001

STEVE CASE
CHAIRMAN
AOL TIME WARNER

PLAY OF THE YEAR: Case had the victory of his career when he consummated the AOL–Time Warner deal in December, making him the pre-eminent figure in the digital convergence, the man who reigns over an unprecedented colossus with the dominant position in the old media as well as the new. AOL Time Warner is truly omnipresent, probably the first company that the average citizen will encounter every day of his life. Case's coup is especially impressive considering that he pulled it off under the worst possible circumstances: he used a highly inflated Net stock to buy the world's biggest media company, and he kept the deal together even after the Internet bubble burst, tech stocks were worth far less, and it was glaringly obvious that Time Warner's extraordinary assets were being taken on the cheap. Since the merger, Case has kept a very low profile. Rather than

In 2000, and again in 2001, *Vanity Fair* named me the most powerful person of the New Establishment, ahead of Bill Gates, Steve Jobs, Warren Buffett, Jeff Bezos, and others. The coronation didn't last long. Two years later, I had fallen off the list completely.

Riding horses with Ted Turner at his ranch in Montana, a few months after the AOL Time Warner merger. Ted soon turned against me, and lobbied for my resignation as chairman.

A celebratory night at the Grammy Awards in 2002, with current Time Warner CEO Jeff Bewkes and former CEO Dick Parsons. The smiles belied the growing frustrations that led to my resignation months later.

Eric Luse, San Francisco Chronicle

Hugging my brother Dan at the Hambrecht & Quist healthcare conference in 2002. Sadly, he died of brain cancer a few months later. It felt like my worlds were starting to come apart.

Case Foundation

The work of The Case Foundation has taken us all over the world. Here I am with my wife Jean in a remote village in Ethiopia in 2005.

Back at AOL's Virginia headquarters in 2010, as AOL celebrates its 25th anniversary. It was a long, unpredictable, extraordinary, and sometimes strange ride. Looking back, I'll always be grateful for the pioneers who believed in the idea of the Internet when most were skeptical.

Disembarking from *Air Force One* after flying with President Obama to Cleveland to launch Startup America in 2011.

Huddling with GE CEO Jeff Immelt to discuss entrepreneurship as we wait for President Obama to address the nation at the U.S. Capitol in 2011.

Discussing philanthropy with Warren Buffett and Bill Gates in 2012 at the Forbes 400 Summit. Warren helped me think through my next act—starting Revolution, an investment company. After duking it out for a decade, it has been a pleasure working with Bill on initiatives such as The Giving Pledge.

Joining with four senators to announce the bipartisan Startup Act 2.0 in 2012 (from left, Senator Mark Warner, me, and Senators Marco Rubio, Jerry Moran, and Chris Coons).

Watching President Obama sign the Jumpstart Our Business Startups Act with Majority Leader Eric Cantor, other members of Congress, and entrepreneurs in the Rose Garden of the White House in 2012. It was a moment to celebrate: both parties came together to pass pro-entrepreneurship legislation.

Disembarking from *Air Force One* with President Obama as we spread the "Rise of the Rest" message about regional entrepreneurship.

We've traversed 4,000 miles and visited 19 U.S. cities by bus as part of our effort to promote regional entrepreneurship. We kicked off the effort in Detroit—a city that was the Silicon Valley of its day, fell on hard times, and is beginning to show signs of a comeback. From left: Entrepreneur Dan Gilbert and Michigan Governor Rick Snyder.

Our Rise of the Rest team celebrates the completion of another bus trip, this time in New Orleans.

During every Rise of the Rest bus stop, we host a pitch competition for local entrepreneurs. The winner in Pittsburgh receives a $100,000 check from me and fellow judge Franco Harris.

Discussing the need for immigration reform with President Obama at the White House in 2013. Immigration policy is complex and can be emotionally charged, but we need to come together to pass bipartisan reform so we can continue to win what is now a global battle for talent.

My focus in recent years has been on investing in and mentoring the next generation of entrepreneurs. Here I am with the founders of Sweetgreen, a fast casual restaurant that is providing healthier options. Revolution invested $40 million, and I joined the board.

While our Rise of the Rest initiative is focused principally on lifting up entrepreneurial regions within the U.S., we also have visited Africa, the Middle East, and Cuba hoping to spawn startup cultures. Here we are with the Andela fellows in Lagos, Nigeria, in 2015.

AP Photo/Charles Dharapak

Dinner at the White House in 2014 with President Obama. I attended high school with "Barry" Obama in Hawaii in the mid-1970s. Thirty years later we reconnected when he became a senator and moved to Washington DC.

Joanne S. Lawton © Washington Business Journal

In the past decade my investment firm Revolution has invested in nearly 100 entrepreneurs. We focus those investments on people and ideas that can change the world.

entrepreneurship, they didn't need our money; they needed our help. In partnership with the Kauffman Foundation, we built a coalition with broad support from more than a dozen corporations, and launched it in dozens of startup regions. When impact investors needed help changing rules to allow retirement funds to invest in impact funds, they needed an advocate. We joined with the National Advisory Board on Impact Investing to push for changes, and a key rule was altered in 2015.

When we do invest money in this space, we work across sectors. While The Case Foundation builds support for impact investment, we have become impact investors ourselves. I remember Jean giving a talk at the South by Southwest conference in 2014. She was there representing The Case Foundation, and I was in the audience representing Revolution, my investment firm. As she walked through her presentation, she came to a set of slides that highlighted some high-impact companies that were poised to break out in the space. As she talked through her list, she landed on a company I was particularly intrigued by—Revolution Foods.

REVOLUTION FOODS

Revolution Foods (of no relation to my investment firm) was founded in 2006 by Kristin Groos Richmond and Kirsten Saenz Tobey. Both worked in public schools, and both were understandably frustrated by the cafeteria offerings. As entrepreneurs, they saw an opportunity to change the system of providing food to schools, particularly in underserved areas. It was a chance to have a positive impact on student health in a $20 billion market.

What they were witnessing was the outcome of a deeply dysfunctional food system, one in which "big food" companies spend billions of dollars to feed our kids fat, salt, and sugar to pad their bottom lines. The school system was a victim of the greater food system failure, which has led to the highest rate of obesity among children anywhere in the world—an entire generation put on the path to chronic disease before they're even old enough to make healthy choices for themselves.

"This is an obesity crisis," Betti Wiggins, executive director of Detroit Public Schools' Office of Nutrition, told the *New York Times*. "And we've gotten rid of health classes and P.E., so we're back to the lunch lady and the tray."

To fight this crisis, Revolution Foods' founders started a school meal company. They were convinced it was possible to provide healthy and affordable food that kids actually liked, and they believed they could also expand this promise to families by distributing their food into grocery stores. They set out to prove it.

As we were leaving the SXSW conference, I decided to reach out to Revolution Foods to see if they were planning to raise money. Their initial investor was Nancy Pfund, a long-time friend of ours and a pioneer in impact investing. On the foundation side, we were eager to showcase impact investing as a new frontier. And on the investment side, we had made a strategic decision at my investment firm to focus on the future of food. I emailed Nancy that afternoon, and she connected us to the company. A few months later, our Revolution Growth fund closed on a $30 million investment. In 2015, we invested another $15 million.

CONVERGENCE

Impact investing is still in its infancy. In 2013, an estimated $50 billion went toward impact investing, while global wealth sat at over $150 trillion. But a change is afoot. One projection suggests that impact investing will rise twenty-fold by 2020, to more than $1 trillion. It's also become the focus of some of major institutional players. The world's largest asset management firm, the ten largest investment banks, and several major private equity investors have all recently developed specific teams, funds, and pools of capital devoted to impact investing. It's no longer a boutique affair.

Instead, what we are seeing is the convergence of three powerful megatrends—the Third Wave, the rise of the rest, and impact investing—and the chance for a supercharged result. As market incentives continue to drive each of these phenomena, the landscape will change profoundly. Because if Third Wave entrepreneurs, funded by committed impact investors, build successful companies in rise-of-the-rest cities, an economic transformation isn't just possible; it's inevitable.

NINE

A MATTER OF TRUST

OWARD THE end of 1999, AOL was in an enviable position. We had more than 22 million subscribers,[1] up from only 1 million in 1994,[2] an exponential growth rate matched only by our rising stock price. When we went public in 1992, our market value was about $70 million. By October 1997, it was $8 billion.[3] Nine months later, we were worth three times as much.[4] And by the time we announced the merger with Time Warner in January 2000, a mere eighteen months later, we were valued at $163 billion.[5] AOL ended up being the best-performing stock of the 1990s.

The market was declaring us the victor of the Internet, and to the victor went the spoils. The surge in value gave us ample capital. We decided to use stock to make a number of acquisitions. One of the highest-profile among them was our purchase of Netscape for $4.2 billion. The Silicon Valley–based company had rocketed to a leadership position on the strength of its web browsing software. Its wunderkind founder, Marc Andreessen, had become one of the most successful young entrepreneurs of the time. After AOL acquired Netscape, Marc moved to Virginia to become the CTO of AOL, reporting directly to me. He stayed for a year, then returned to California, where he would start a software company and later a venture capital firm with Ben Horowitz, a fellow Netscape executive. Acquiring companies like Netscape improved our overall market position, but we soon realized we needed to do more. We needed to lock in the value we created, while further diversifying the business.

After some lengthy deliberations, we came up with a few options for our next move. We decided to go big—to try to pull off a large, transformational merger while our stock was riding high, to lock in shareholder gains while we expanded our strategic reach. We spent months analyzing a range of options.

We could expand further into content, we concluded, by acquiring a company like Disney. We could deepen our communications offerings by merging with a company like AT&T. Or we could double down on the Internet by acquiring companies like eBay and Electronic Arts. We pursued all of those paths simultaneously—having merger discussions with each of those companies, along with many others.

Financial considerations helped guide our hand. Our stock had skyrocketed twenty-fold in less than three years, and we worried that the Internet mania might end. So buying other businesses that would expand our portfolio and put a floor under our valuation was key. But we didn't just want to hedge any potential financial downside. We also wanted to maximize our strategic upside.

Buying more content had appeal. We believed that as broadband took hold, the value of media brands and especially video would increase. Hence the interest in Disney. But while we were intrigued, we were concerned that as barriers to entry lowered over time, content would become commoditized, leading to an eventual decline in the value of media brands.

Expanding our communications offerings made some sense. AOL had always been, first and foremost, about connecting people. Our success with AOL Instant Messenger made us the dominant player in online messaging, and we figured we could leverage that into a full suite of communications offerings (remember, this was years before Skype and more than a decade before WhatsApp was released). A storied American brand like AT&T would also enhance our credibility as we expanded globally. But the communications path seemed risky. We expected AT&T's core revenue stream—long-distance calls—to be eroded by new technologies, including our own.

Acquiring other Internet companies had its appeal, although it felt like the safe path. We would have partners who were culturally aligned and who shared our conviction about the Internet's potential, making the post-merger company easier to manage. We initiated M&A discussions with eBay and Electronic Arts. In fact, when we were negotiating with Time

Warner, Meg Whitman, who had taken eBay from startup to global force in just a few short years, was waiting in an adjacent conference room at our headquarters in Virginia. Had the negotiation deteriorated with Time Warner, we were prepared to close an acquisition deal with her.

But doubling down on the Internet was counter to our goal of diversifying. These other Internet companies were highly valued, too, and if the stock market took a turn against tech, our combined company would likely be eviscerated.

ENTER TIME WARNER

In the end, it was fairly clear that the best merger partner would be Time Warner. In many ways, the company had everything we needed. Time Warner had been formed a decade earlier through the merger of two media giants, Time Inc. and Warner Communications. Time Inc. was co-founded in the 1920s by a young entrepreneur named Henry Luce, who, in the process of selling *Time, Life, Sports Illustrated,* and *Fortune* to a growing, educated middle class, became the most influential publisher of the mid-twentieth century. Warner Communications had been built by Steve Ross, a charismatic company builder who went from owning parking garages to assembling one of the world's largest media companies, which included the Warner Brothers movie studio, the industry-leading Warner Music company, and a range of other content businesses, including Lorimar-Telepictures. Later, Time and Warner (by then renamed Time Warner) also acquired Turner Broad-casting, led by the energetic, if idiosyncratic, Ted Turner. By the time we started contemplating a merger with them, Time Warner had serious heft—nearly $30 billion of revenue and $8 billion of profits. It had a trove of content brands—Time Inc., HBO, CNN, TBS, Warner Brothers, Warner Music, and many others. And it owned Time Warner Cable, one of the largest cable companies, so we would have a clear path to broadband, something we believed essential.

Broadband was coming, and, with it, a major threat to our dial-up–driven business. (In a world of smartphones, it's amazing to think back to a time, less than fifteen years ago, when you couldn't use the Internet and your phone at the same time!) Instead of phone lines, broadband used cable lines that we didn't have open access to—and couldn't get access to our-selves. Cable companies didn't have to share their broadband lines the way phone companies had to with their dial-up lines. The regulations made it possible for them to shut out their competition altogether.

The "open access" fight, as it became known in the late 1990s, was a preview of the net neutrality fight that would come much later. Both dealt with the question of whether the owner of the "pipes"—the wire into your home—can control what you see over the Internet. During the open access battle, the cable companies took the view that they could just say no, refusing access to companies like AOL. During the net neutral-ity fight, they were subtler; they no longer sought to lock out competition, but they did seek to disadvantage it. They took the view that they could simply make some sites perform less well, unless those sites paid an extra fee to the cable company. And, in fact, when Tom Wheeler, chairman of the Federal Communications Commission (FCC), approved the commission's net neutrality rules in 2015, he cited his fights with me in those early days as having been instructive to his decision.

We urged the government to intervene, giving us the same access to broadband as we had to phone lines. I spoke wherever and to whomever I could, whether to members of the FCC, members of Congress, or presidential candidates. In fact, when then-governor George W. Bush was campaigning in Virginia, I met with him to make my case for open access. He listened to what I had to say, and he had his aides follow up. But about a month later, he came out against our proposal, arguing that the market could sort the issue out without government intervention. In retrospect, he was probably right. But that he was not willing to take a stand was unhelpful, and it was one of the key factors that made a merger with Time Warner seem not just sensible but necessary. If we couldn't partner with a cable company, the thinking went, maybe we needed to buy one. And Time Warner had both a large broadband footprint and a number of valuable other brands and businesses. We concluded that we needed Time Warner. And we thought Time Warner needed us.

The content companies—HBO, Turner Broadcasting System (TBS), Warner Brothers—had a lot to gain from the digital delivery of their product. The print journalism companies, which were already in the throes of an irrevocable, Internet-induced transformation, risked rapid decline if they didn't incorporate an aggressive digital strategy into their business model. The video entertainment businesses would have a way to distribute their content digitally—and, over time, directly—to consumers, bypassing distribution intermediaries. And Time Warner Cable would have the chance to become the biggest company in the industry, giving them numerous synergies to wring out of a merger with AOL. They would control the pipeline of access that brought consumers to the Internet, the platform consumers used to explore it, and the content they consumed on it.

Together, AOL and Time Warner would have what seemed like the perfect platform. But there was one big question: Could we get them to agree? Most insiders assumed that there was no way they would ever consider it. Our bankers suggested we not even bother trying.

I decided to give it a shot.

THE BEGINNING OF A COURTSHIP

I was hoping to enter into a negotiation with Time Warner CEO Jerry Levin on a lot more than price. In combining two different companies, we'd have to come to terms on a range of issues, from operational structure to strategic priorities. And at the top of that list was a threshold question we would have to get past in order to move on to more important matters: Who would run the merged company?

I was reluctant to give up control over AOL, which I had watched grow—and helped build—into a company beyond anything I could have imagined. It was like my child. I was confident it had a bright future—brighter still, I thought, if we could execute the merger.

At the same time, I understood enough about Jerry to know that he would never go for it if he wasn't to be in charge. It would be hard enough for executives at Time Warner to accept that AOL, still relatively young, had a significantly higher valuation than they did; it would be impossible to convince them to give me the power to run the combined company.

I decided, before picking up the phone to call Jerry, that I would offer to step aside as CEO so that he could run the merged entity. And that was the first thing I told him when he answered the phone, in the same sentence in which I asked him to consider the merger. There was a long pause. "Let's have dinner," he finally responded.

Later, in an interview in April 2001, David Frost asked Jerry and me about our "courtship." I guess you could say that this dinner was our first big date, and it went well. Jerry saw the potential of technology and was doing his best impression of Paul Revere inside his company: "The Internet is coming! The Internet is coming!" But all of his attempts to get people in line and marshal a change—to attack rather than defend—had fallen flat. In the mid-1990s Jerry spent more than $100 million on internal digital efforts like Pathfinder, a web portal that was supposed to be a one-stop shop for Time Warner content. But it never went anywhere, largely because of internal squabbles over turf. This merger was his chance to get Time Warner equipped for the Internet age.

But over the next several months, in conversations about organization and exchange ratios (essentially the price of the acquisition), the negotiations often looked more like a couple on the verge of a breakup rather than one ready to get married. Both sides walked away multiple times.

There was a point in November 1999 when I was on a panel at Time Inc.'s headquarters with Ted Turner and Richard Branson, the founder of Virgin Group. After we all finished speaking, Ted and I walked out onto the patio. As the vice chair of Time Warner's board (and its largest individual shareholder), Ted knew about the proposed merger—and that we were at an impasse. He urged me to keep at it. "Steve, we should make this work," he said, putting his arm around my shoulder. "You need us and we need you. Let's figure out a way to get a deal done. Don't give up."

I followed his advice. We kept on negotiating among a small group of executives, in order to keep the number of decision makers within reasonable limits and to prevent the discussions from leaking. Had it leaked, both of our stock prices would have been affected, and merging could have easily become unfeasible. Negotiating this way ultimately led to a good deal at the right price. But it also meant that some of the most senior executives at Time Warner, including several who were running entire businesses within Time Warner, only found out about the deal the night before we announced it. Many were frustrated—indeed, blindsided and embarrassed—and the animosity lingered, poisoning a lot of what we had planned to achieve together.

Should we have approached the negotiation differently? I don't think so. There's no doubt that, had we come to terms in a way that involved consensus from all senior executives, there would have been more support and less anger. But I have trouble believing that we could have come to consensus with such a large group, or that a group that size could have kept the negotiations private. As I and many other CEOs have found in the past, opposition inside the room often finds expression outside the room, sometimes in the form of a leak to a reporter. I believed then, and still believe, that we had to protect the integrity of the deal. And I was convinced we would have the time and space to rebuild any bridges we'd burned.

Besides, other than bruised egos, the Time Warner executives had little to complain about. I tried to take the high road, describing the merger in the press and elsewhere as a "merger of equals." But the truth was, it was anything but. At the time of the merger, we were the younger company, sure, but with a market cap of $163 billion, we were worth more than General Motors and Ford combined. The deal was structured as an acquisition of Time Warner by AOL. AOL shareholders went from owning 100 percent of a company that generated $5 billion of revenue and $1 billion of profit to owning 55 percent of a more diversified company that was expected to generate nearly $40 billion of revenue and $10 billion of profit. We paid a 70 percent premium, and we let Time Warner executives accelerate their vesting period, so they could sell their stock and get a windfall. And, in fact, some did. Those who didn't stayed by choice. They believed in what we were doing.

THE BIGGEST MERGER IN HISTORY

On Saturday, January 8, 2000, we came to terms on the deal. I flew to New York the next day to prepare for a major press conference. We were announcing the merger Monday morning. It was surreal.

The AOL executive managing our communications effort was Kenny Lerer (who would later go on to co-found the *Huffington Post*). He knew the Time Warner culture because he had worked with them in the past, and I remember him saying to me, "Tomorrow, when this is announced, your life is going to change, and not in a good way."

"Why is that?" I asked.

"Because you're going to go from being the CEO of a really hot company to being a chairman without any of the businesses reporting to you. AOL's not even reporting to you. You'll have a nice title, but no operating responsibilities, and people will start ignoring you. You've gotten used to being in the front seat driving, but now you'll be in the back seat watching."

I didn't have a moment of hesitation about the deal we were announcing. I was confident it was the right thing to do for AOL and its shareholders, and I was well aware of the difference in job responsibilities between a chairman, who runs board meetings, and a CEO, who runs the actual company. Nonetheless, Kenny's certainty surprised me. Particularly his closing remark: "At the press conference tomorrow, just don't look like you got the raw end of the stick when you go out there, or people will assume you got shoved aside."

In the end, I think I may have overcompensated. I was determined to give people the impression that I was the victor, not the one losing out. On front pages of newspapers across the country were pictures of me pumping my fist into the sky like I'd won a gold medal, a giant smile on my face.

My performance worked. Almost too well, actually. Within a few days of the announcement, it looked like AOL was taking over the world. I remember landing at Dulles Airport, seeing my face on the cover of what seemed like just about every magazine on the newsstand. That week felt like AOL's coming-of-age—as if the Internet had finally arrived. And yet, in retrospect, ratcheting up my performance gave the false impression that I was running the combined company. And that exacerbated the perception later that it was mostly my fault that the combined company was faltering. I had ceded my operating responsibility but none of the accountability for the company's performance. And it wouldn't be long before problems emerged.

The day we launched, we filled the press release with bold promises for our shared future. "AOL Time Warner Will Be Premier Global Company Delivering Branded Information, Entertainment, and Communications Across Rapidly Converging Media Platforms and Changing Technology," we declared.[6] That was the vision. That was what we believed we were building, and what our collective shareholders—98 percent of whom voted for the merger—embraced. But that is not where we ended up. And the internal and external problems that would undo the company were already taking shape.

The first was internal. As part of the merger, we had committed to $1 billion worth of cost cuts across the company. My sense at the time was that it was a reasonable target. The combined companies had costs of about $30 billion, so we were talking about trimming 3 percent. But the decision forced layoffs and reprioritization among the businesses in the first months after the merger.

"I now have to cut people and projects because of this merger," frustrated executives would say. "And I wouldn't have had to otherwise."

That bred an immediate and spiraling resentment among senior executives and severely undercut our ability to build trust. There was rising tension about the merger, even before the stock market took its tumble.

THE BUBBLE BURSTS

Exactly two months to the day after announcing the merger, the NASDAQ hit its all-time high.[7] Then the dot-com bubble collapsed. Our valuation plummeted. In the year to come, we would lose nearly 80 percent of our value. But the crash didn't just hurt our valuation; it decimated the 401(k) plans of Time Warner employees who were already embarrassed that an upstart had taken them over. Now they were angry. It created a climate that, for some, confirmed—and even exacerbated—fears about and biases against the merger. You could feel the tide turning in the headlines, but it was nothing compared to the shift in posture among Time Warner executives, many of whom were already suspicious about the Internet's potential. The plummeting market was bringing out the skeptic in everyone. And you don't want to get in the way of a bear market when she's protecting her cubs.

But even after such a drastic market correction, we were still positioned well. Would it have been better for AOL Time Warner had the Internet had a few more years of boom? Sure. Do I think it would have made a difference? Absolutely. A rising stock price might have convinced the media (and more of our executives) that the merger was a good idea, or at least given us the time and the credibility to better integrate the two companies.

By the same token, I'm skeptical that more time would have produced a meaningfully different result. In the end, what did us in was that we were trying to join two companies that were incompatible in structure, in culture, and in mission. From an organizational perspective, Time Warner operated like a portfolio of independent companies—with Turner Broadcasting, Time Inc., HBO, Warner Brothers, New Line Cinema, Warner Music, and Time Warner Cable all operating largely autonomously. The result was rule by fiefdom. Rupert Murdoch once told me that it was easier for News Corp to get a deal with Time Warner Cable than it was for HBO. And they were part of the same company! And because the individual businesses that made up Time Warner functioned independently, AOL wasn't really merging with Time Warner—it was engaged in nearly a dozen different mergers *simultaneously*.

From a cultural perspective, there was an enormous and fundamental disconnect between AOL and much of Time Warner about the potential of the Internet. Several top executives who had been at Time Warner for decades believed the Internet to be overhyped and had a large constituency within the company who agreed.

The *Wall Street Journal* quoted Time Warner executives as saying I was too focused on "shaky theories about convergence of technology and entertainment." What they thought unlikely, we knew was inevitable—and coming soon. Once speeds were fast enough, there was no reason why HBO's shows, for example, needed to be limited to one platform. But back then, the idea of a streaming HBO GO app would have seemed downright ludicrous to many of the executives at HBO.

In May 2000, Jerry announced a new management structure, and it sent shock waves through the company. When I'd first talked to Ted Turner about the idea of the merger, he had loved it. He thought that Time Warner was too bureaucratic and slow-moving, and he was convinced that the merger would shake things up. But in May, Jerry decided that Ted should remain vice chairman but should no longer have a day-to-day operational role at the Turner Broadcasting division. Ted was out—and he was angry. He viewed the decision as an affront to his self-worth. When the stock plunged and he started losing billions, he boiled over. His temper exploded frequently at board meetings, and he used whatever opportunity he could to direct venom and vitriol our way. He wanted Jerry gone (and would soon want me gone, too), and he wasn't shy about it.

Disagreement generated discord, not just between Ted and Jerry but throughout the company. The environment became toxic. To this day, I am still surprised by what people did out of embarrassment or anger, how petty the situation became. Instead of discussing how we could work together to put properties like *Time* on a path of sustained success in a digital future, people were more interested in bitter debates over whether or not *Time* reporters should use AOL's email service. At times it seemed that no matter where you turned in the company, you'd find contentious arguments and needless sniping over little disagreements, resulting in near-total neglect of the bigger picture.

I was hopeful that Jerry would be effective as CEO in

bringing people together to execute our vision. But as smart as Jerry is, he couldn't sell the idea throughout the company, and I underestimated how much mistrust there already was within Time Warner. People from the various divisions of the company just weren't coming together. The companies were so isolated from one another that AOL never even got access to Time Warner's broadband infrastructure, the easiest deliverable of the entire merger. AOL had the biggest Internet brand in the world, but the executives at Time Warner Cable wanted to continue doing things their own way, on their own.

I grew increasingly frustrated that Jerry wasn't making enough of an effort to deliver broadband to AOL, or to push the other key strategic initiatives made possible by the merger. But things really boiled over when I learned that he was starting to pursue another acquisition, this time of AT&T's broadband system. We hadn't even figured out how to manage what we already had, and Jerry was looking to add more complexity.

It was aggravating. "If we're not doing any of the things that the merger was supposed to do, why the hell did we do it to begin with?" I asked him.

"You know what, Steve," he shouted back, "I ask myself that question every single day."

THE QUIET COUP

Less than a year after the merger's approval, it was clear to me that to save it, we needed a change in leadership and direction.

In truth, the fault did not lie solely with Jerry or the Time Warner executives. There was a swagger and arrogance to some of the AOL executives that created problems. And I wasn't as engaged as I needed to be. I made the calculation that it was better not to spend too much time with the management and the divisions so as to avoid creating confusion about who was in charge. But in the end, that distance only crystallized a view that I was arrogant and uninterested.

I needed to make a decision. We needed to replace Jerry. But removing him would require the votes of three-fourths of the board, which meant I would need a consensus candidate to replace him. I knew I couldn't be a candidate myself. I wasn't sure I was up to the challenge, but it didn't matter either way. I knew there was no way I could rally Time Warner executives and board members to support a CEO coming from AOL, and even if we could, Bob Pittman would have been the likeliest option, and that made me uncomfortable. Bob, a media pioneer, had been president and COO of AOL before the merger. He was very numbers-driven, very focused on execution. He'd helped us tighten up our operation, making us more profitable more quickly, which contributed in a very significant way to our skyrocketing stock price. He deserves a lot of credit for that.

At the same time, he was predominantly focused on the short term, sometimes at the expense of the longer view. He was reluctant to do more acquisitions, or make many strategic investments. There was even a time in 1996 when we had the chance to take a 5 percent equity stake in Amazon, a year after it first came online. But Bob refused, pushing through a deal with Barnes & Noble instead—an exclusive with AOL in exchange for tens of millions of dollars up front. It was a classic case of sacrificing long-term strategic value creation for short-term profitability. And so, years later, as I considered how to proceed with Time Warner, I knew that Bob as CEO was a nonstarter. There was only one person who I could imagine getting enough board votes to replace Jerry: Dick Parsons.

Dick had been the president of Time Warner since 1995 and on the board since 1991. He was involved in the merger negotiations and became co-COO with Bob Pittman afterward. Dick was well respected as a manager. Before Time Warner, he'd spent time in government working for Governor and then Vice President Nelson Rockefeller, and he was the president of Dime Savings Bank. He was accomplished, trusted, and well liked, and in many ways, he was already being groomed as Jerry's successor.

From the beginning, I wondered if Dick was the right person to lead the company. He was smart, and he had a great way with people. But he was old-school. He didn't handle his own emails, let alone use a computer—and it's tough to understand technology if you don't engage with it. Dick knew this—by his own admission, he wasn't a "vision" guy, particularly when it came to the Internet. He was there to craft partnerships, comfort regulators, and settle disagreements among strong-willed executives. He was political—a diplomat, not a disruptor. His

A *Matter of Trust*

preference was to settle things down rather than shake them up—even as the world changed all around him. Given the lack of options, however, I felt that whether or not Dick was the right person was somewhat immaterial. The status quo was unworkable, and we needed a different direction. Dick was the only person who could muster the requisite support. And I was confident I could partner with Dick; I could take the lead on the strategy, and he could drive the day-to-day execution.

It was settled. Over a weekend in early December 2001, I reached out to Dick to convey my growing concerns about Jerry's leadership and to let him know I planned to talk to board members about removing Jerry as CEO and promoting Dick to fill the role. I told Dick that I would be much more engaged, working hand in hand with him to get things back on track. He understood and was supportive. He and I made dozens of calls to various directors over a single weekend in an effort to secure the votes. By the time Jerry learned of our efforts, it was too late. He knew what was coming. A few days later, he announced his retirement. He was gone by May. And it wasn't long before I missed him.

A few months after Dick was named CEO, I set up a dinner with the two of us and Lou Gerstner, then the CEO of IBM. I was pushing Dick to be more strategic and drive more integration throughout the company, and I thought that Lou, who had done the same at IBM, would be a helpful voice in that conversation.

We met at an Italian restaurant in New York's West Village.

133

After about an hour, Dick excused himself from the table to use the restroom. As soon as he was gone, Lou turned to me and whispered, "Boy, Steve, you sure have your work cut out for you with Dick." He was shocked by how little Dick seemed to understand about technology.

"Why do you think I set up this dinner?" I replied. "I feel like we need an intervention."

AOL THE ORPHAN

Not long after the meeting, Dick decided to reorganize the company. His plan was to have half of the company report to Jeff Bewkes, CEO of HBO, and the other half report to Time Inc. CEO Don Logan. Under Dick's plan, both AOL and Time Warner Cable would be part of Don's portfolio.

I opposed this structure. It's not that I didn't respect Don. On the contrary, I thought that he was an excellent publishing executive. My problem was that Don didn't have a deep understanding of digital technology, and he hated the Internet. He had referred to it as a "black hole"—as in, money goes in and it doesn't come out. And he, along with Jeff, had been among the noisiest antagonists after the merger, angry that AOL had gotten the deal done, and seemingly eager to get retribution.

If Dick put AOL, the Internet's premier platform of the decade, and Time Warner Cable, one of the company's most tech-centric businesses, in the hands of someone who didn't believe the Internet had much of a future, he could end up destroying both. I made this very point to Dick, Jeff, and Don over dinner. I suggested some organizational alternatives. But it was clear that my opinion didn't really matter.

We talked about changing the name of the company, but not about changing its culture. The perception was that it couldn't be done. Maybe that was right, but the reality was, almost no one was interested in trying. Not that I didn't make the effort. After Dick took over, I got an apartment in New York and started spending a lot more time at headquarters— and a lot more time with Dick. And I pushed to create a strategy committee, made up of leaders from each division, which I chaired. We made some progress, and outlined a handful of initiatives, but after six months it became clear that the committee members didn't have the support of the executives above them—or of Dick as the new CEO. At one point, Jeff Bewkes blasted me during a strategy committee meeting. He panned AOL as being the division "most off its plan." He directed his vitriol at me, even though he knew it had been more than a year since I'd had any direct authority over AOL. It was maddening; I was sidelined, watching my "baby" being weakened by fuzzy strategy and poor execution, yet I was the one being blamed for the predictably poor results.

Not surprisingly, the clash of culture wasn't limited to the management team. There were heated discussions in board meetings. Half of the merged company's board came from AOL and the other half from Time Warner, and they remained largely warring camps. Neither side seemed to really listen to the other. We were often talking past each other, when we even talked at all.

As chairman of the board, I was accountable without having much authority, culpable without real control. I had gone from being the CEO of one of the hottest companies in the world, leading a board and a management team, to being something of a pariah with waning influence. And meanwhile, the company's self-inflicted wounds kept accruing. There was a time, for example, when AOL wanted to add voice services to AIM, our instant messaging service. On the AOL side, we knew there was big market potential in doing so—a view confirmed a few years later when Skype launched in 2003. But Time Warner Cable was promoting a "Triple Play" digital package at the time, and they didn't want anything to interfere with it. Eventually the cable guys succeeded in squashing AOL's new services because they believed they could get a higher margin in the short term, in essence killing a new business to protect an existing one.

In February 2002, I attended the Grammys. Ahmet Ertegun, the legendary music executive who founded Atlantic Records (which, by then, was part of Warner Music), heard I was coming and asked for a private meeting with me. We sat in a corner of the Peninsula hotel in Beverly Hills and talked about the state of our businesses. He shared his frustration with Warner Music, his disappointment about no longer being consulted. He was a hero of mine—an icon of the music business (indeed, a member of the Rock and Roll Hall of Fame). It was sad to hear. What was sadder, perhaps, was that I felt the exact same way. I was increasingly isolated, increasingly powerless, and yet shouldering much of the blame, both in private and public. I wanted to intervene to help Ahmet, but I had no real ability to do so by then.

In the midst of this turmoil, the merger was hit with some very bad press. In July 2002, our hometown paper, the *Washington Post*, ran a couple of very harsh and negative stories about AOL. They were about the culture—excesses in personality and behavior when AOL was the dominant Internet company of the late 1990s. But one, which ran under the headline "Unconventional Transactions Boosted Sales," raised the claim that AOL had made errors in accounting. Coming at a time when the merged AOL Time Warner was foundering, and Time Warner legacy executives were looking to blame whatever they could on the AOL team, the stories provided an opportunity for many people inside and outside of the company to seize on these claims as evidence that Time Warner had been "hoodwinked" into merging with AOL.

There were three problems with this notion. First, virtually all of the specific transactions cited by the *Post* (and by a later SEC investigation) as reflecting improper accounting had occurred *after* the AOL Time Warner merger deal. So the transactions and their accounting could not have "misled" Time Warner into merging with AOL, because they happened after Time Warner agreed to the merger (mostly during the year-long period between the merger agreement and the deal's closing). Second, though this scandal took place against a backdrop of a period during which several big companies got in trouble for accounting on transactions that were made up, the problems with AOL's accounting were nothing of that sort. The transactions called out by critics and reviewed by the SEC were real deals involving real payments to AOL—but with some debate about how the payments were labeled.

And third, the transactions didn't really add up to all that much. The sum total of these deals amounted to a few percent of AOL's total revenues. As *Slate* wrote in August 2002, under the reading line "What did AOL's accountants do wrong? Not much": "The thing to bear in mind is that even the worst-case scenario—that AOL had no business booking the revenue as its own but did anyway—isn't especially serious."

Still, the damage was done. With the media frenzy about accounting issues at companies like Enron in 2002, and the widespread criticism of the merger, it was all fuel on a burning fire. I knew we had to do something, but with little remaining influence over the management team, I focused my efforts on swaying the board instead. I distributed a memo outlining a wide range of strategic moves that I thought merited consideration. I suggested that we consider buying Google, back when it was worth $2 billion, long before it went public. (We already owned 5 percent of Google, which AOL obtained in exchange for integrating Google search within the service. Today, that stake would be worth upwards of $20 billion.) I also floated the idea of buying Apple, to benefit from their expertise in software, hardware, and design. These suggestions, and many others, were dismissed or ignored. It was clear I was out of options.

It was time for me to go.

TAKING STOCK

The year we were trying to get the merger approved, several companies asked the government to block the deal, arguing that the combined company would be so powerful that no one would be able to compete. It turned out we couldn't get out of our own way. Three years after our competitors marched on Washington to stop us, we stopped ourselves. We had terrific assets—and a great group of executives. But it was a little like the 2004 Olympics: You put together what should have been a dream team, only to go on to lose to Puerto Rico and Lithuania.

There were factors like the stock market meltdown that played a role. But mostly, it came down to people. It came down to emotions and egos and, ultimately, the culture itself. That something with the potential to be the first trillion-dollar company could end up losing $200 billion in value[8] should tell you just how important the people factor is. It doesn't really matter what the plan is if you can't get your people aligned around achieving the same objectives. As Jim Collins once wrote, "you not only need the right people on the bus, but you also need the right people in the right seats."

In 2015, *Fortune* held its Global Forum in San Francisco, the very same event I had attended in Shanghai in 1999. The comments almost uniformly made the case that culture is critical. "Fifty percent of our business has changed in the last ten years," said Joe Kaeser, CEO of Siemens. "The key to surviving is having an ownership culture. You have to get to people's hearts. You have to get to people's pride."

"The culture is the one thing I've got to get right," added Brian Roberts, CEO of Comcast. Mark Bertolini, CEO of Aetna, agreed: "Culture does trump strategy, every day."

At the time of the merger, I didn't fully appreciate how much of a role personal emotions could play in professional decisions. In retrospect, I was naïve to think that strategic moves that seemed obvious to me would be equally obvious to others. For example, I was confident that the best approach for the company was to embrace technology and new business models, and was shocked when my attempts to encourage investment in Napster and other early pioneering digital services were soundly rejected. I didn't appreciate the work it would take to convince the company's executives of things that seemed so clear to me. In one board meeting, I even noted that the two sides seemed to be speaking different languages and speaking past each other. And while some of the differences related to different world views and strategic perspectives, I think much of it, sadly, related to personal mistrust and lingering resentments.

I could have done a better job of managing that mistrust. I could have done a better job of repairing burned bridges and establishing meaningful working relationships with those who treated me with such skepticism. And I could have done a better job of making it clear that I wanted to be part of the solution. My plan, from the beginning, was to take a step back, to make sure people knew that Jerry was the one making the decisions. But in hindsight, I think I stepped too far back. That was in part the result of circumstances in my personal life: Three years before the merger, my first wife and I divorced, which led me to want to devote more time to my children. And just six months after the merger was announced, doctors diagnosed my brother Dan with terminal brain cancer. He didn't have much time left. I bought a house on his block in San Francisco, and visited frequently in the fifteen months before he died. I don't regret spending the time I needed with my family. But I do regret not spending more time with key executives. What I intended to be good for the company— staying out of the way—looked to some like arrogance, even indifference.

Perhaps we could have brought in an outside CEO to replace Jerry. But that wasn't really possible in practice. I'm certain my efforts to oust Jerry would have failed if I hadn't proposed Dick as his replacement. When I floated the idea of trying to buy Apple later, I had a side agenda: bringing Steve Jobs into the company, with the thought that perhaps he could eventually become CEO. He had the credibility and skill in the tech and digital worlds, and because of the success of Pixar, he also had the trust of content creators, particularly in Hollywood. I still like that idea, but there were never the votes for it. It was never even seriously discussed.

In the end, resigning from AOL Time Warner was hard. Soon after the merger was announced, *Vanity Fair* had ranked me the most powerful person of the "new establishment," ahead of Bill Gates, Rupert Murdoch, Warren Buffett, and Steve Jobs. A couple years later, I wasn't even on the list. I went from running one of the most celebrated companies in the country to not running anything, and being publicly embarrassed. It was not a happy time in my life. I spent much of it reflecting on what had gone so right—and so wrong—and about what I should do next.

A week after stepping down, I met with Donn Davis, who had been an executive at AOL and then my chief of staff when I was chairman of AOL Time Warner. I told him that I wasn't sure precisely what I wanted to do next, but I knew I wanted to get back to my entrepreneurial roots, and I wanted to work with him to help figure out the path forward.

I started making investments later that year and found that I really enjoyed it. There was something empowering and hopeful about using the money I'd made from AOL to back the next generation of entrepreneurs. As the size and scale of those investments picked up, I decided to formalize my efforts by creating an investment firm. I called it Revolution, to signal my desire to back entrepreneurs seeking to revolutionize important aspects of our lives. As our planning efforts accelerated, I reached out to Tige Savage, who had been at Time Warner Ventures, and asked him to join our effort. I made the same ask of David Golden, who had worked for my brother Dan at Hambrecht & Quist, and of Ron Klain, who had been my attorney and had become a trusted counselor. Ted Leonsis later joined us, after he left AOL.

I was putting the band back together to pursue a new dream: building Revolution into one of the world's leading investment companies. I didn't want us to be passive; I wanted to leverage all we had learned to help entrepreneurs succeed. We wouldn't just write checks; we would roll up our sleeves and do everything we could to help the entrepreneurs we backed fulfill their dreams.

We spent the winter of late 2004 and early 2005 preparing to launch. We designed a logo—a stylized red *R* in a black circle—and began to scout businesses and industries. We met with experts and entrepreneurs in a variety of fields. We locked down the domain names and trademarks we wanted. While I had built AOL in what was then a remote part of northern Virginia (and thereby had helped create a whole tech corridor in the outskirts of suburban Virginia), I decided to launch

Revolution in downtown DC, hoping to spur a new tech boom inside this urban hub.

In March 2005, we officially launched Revolution. On launch day, I turned up the speakers at our headquarters and blasted my favorite Steve Earle song, "The Revolution Starts Now."

TEN

THE VISIBLE HAND

'VE NEVER been particularly political. I've always been interested in history and public policy, but I've been independent-minded, not someone comfortable with hyper-partisanship. I studied political science in college, in part because it was the closest thing to marketing that Williams College offered. Even then, so many of the debates we had felt reflexively ideological; people were often polarized and dug in, talking distrustfully past each other. They viewed government in the starkest terms, as either the primary source of our problems or the only solution to them. I could never identify with either of those perspectives, and never liked the black-or-white, win-or-lose style of debate.

Today, when I hear people within the business community talk about government, it often feels like I've gone back in time. If I close my eyes, it's like I'm right back in class, listening to the same arguments—and they're as devoid of nuance as they were all those years ago.

My view is simple: Government is going to be central in the Third Wave. Full stop. It doesn't matter what your view of it is; if you can't figure out how to work with government—and how to get government to work with you—you're likely not going to be a successful Third Wave entrepreneur.

I know that government can often be a problem for businesses. I get that. (Indeed, I have experienced that, many times.) I also understand that entrepreneurs are self-reliant, and not generally inclined to work with government. But the role government plays in shaping our society and our economy will make it a key force in the Third Wave.

After all, it will always be government that defines—either through action or inaction—the environment in which entrepreneurship operates. At its worst, government can be just like the caricature my classmates feared: a hindrance that creates maddening obstacles that hamstring young businesses. But at its best, government can create an environment where innovation and entrepreneurship can thrive, not by providing the certainty of success, but by mitigating risk and expanding the scale of opportunity.

Ultimately, it's government that sets and enforces the rules. Lawmakers decide how easy it ought to be for companies to gain access to global talent and venture capital; how simple it ought to be to start a business and scale it up; how much federal money to invest in research and development, in the creation of new ideas that companies can commercialize. Government determines the ease with which commerce can cross borders and oceans. And often, with instruments like the tax code, government decides which investments to incent and which industries to jump-start.

It is easy to feel frustrated with, even furious about, the dysfunction in Washington. But it's a mistake to conclude that government is useless—or hopeless. The better we understand the critical role that government can—and does—play in the life of a business, the better we can understand that it is our politics, more than our institutions, that are the fundamental problem.

GOVERNMENT AS INNOVATOR

In 1958, the year I was born, President Dwight Eisenhower created an agency called ARPA (Advanced Research Projects Agency, later renamed DARPA; the *D* is for Defense), which was charged with researching beyond-the-horizon ideas. Scientists would have the funding, and the space, to explore new and novel concepts without needing a clear sense of their commercial value—to think beyond short-term profit and imagine long-term transformation. In the years since its creation, DARPA has been responsible for groundbreaking innovations, from stealth plane technology to GPS.

Through initiatives like DARPA, the federal government has often acted as a beating heart for innovation, pumping early energy into nascent ideas that could determine our economic future. It's been a particularly crucial source of support for projects that, in their infancy, lacked a clear commercial use—including the semiconductors that would ultimately drive a technological revolution. Government has often been willing to take risks where the private sector has been afraid to invest. In an assessment of the federal government's influence on technological development, researchers found that from the late '80s through the late '00s, most of the innovations that were recognized with an R&D 100 Award—which is like winning the Academy Award for research and development professionals—relied on federal support at some point in their development.

The fruits of government-funded R&D labor often end up making their way into commercial use. Think about all the work that went into the components that make your computer and smartphone function. A lot of that was made possible because of Cold War–era government investments.[1] The navigation system in your car likely wouldn't exist if the Department of Defense hadn't created a satellite-based global positioning system to improve the nation's nuclear deterrence capabilities.[2] The radar system that guides takeoff and landing every time you board a commercial flight came into existence thanks to naval researchers looking for new methods to detect approaching ships and aircraft.[3] The prescription drugs in your medicine cabinet were likely developed, at least in part, through federal grants.[4,5]

Government was a critical part of AOL's life cycle, too, given the role it played in the creation of the Internet. As early as 1962, ARPA scientists and engineers were talking about the possibility of establishing a network among computers in different locations. Within four years, they began building it. Three years later, they established the first host-to-host connection between computers. And in 1972—a decade after they first conceptualized this network—they sent the first email, and this internetworking system was given its shorthand name: the "Internet."

AOL's success would not have been possible if the government hadn't built the Internet in the first place. Nor would it have been possible if the government hadn't come around to understanding the potential of the Internet placed in private hands and taken the necessary steps to open it up to the public—from the antitrust efforts that led to the Bell System's breakup and increased competition in the telecom market, to the FCC's decision to open telecom networks and enable dial-up access, to Congress's passage of the Telecommunications Act (1996), which helped usher in commercial use of the Internet.

The Internet could have remained a tool for the military and research institutions alone. But government leaders made a crucial decision—to broaden the Internet's scope and allow for its commercialization. This choice seems obvious in retrospect, but it was a visionary act—and an important one. By 2014, the Internet represented $8 trillion in economic activity, a gross domestic product (GDP) larger than Spain's and Canada's, and a faster rate of growth than that of Brazil.

Government's role isn't to commercialize new innovations; it's to push technological advancement forward in areas that the markets won't address on their own—to get ideas and innovations to a point where entrepreneurs with vision can turn them into viable products and businesses. Even seemingly obscure parts of the government can play outsized roles in innovation. The Small Business Administration, for example, makes few headlines, but it's been known to shape headlines. Companies such as Qualcomm, Apple, and Intel all benefited from loan guarantees from the SBA to get off the ground.

Or consider the government-led effort to preserve data and information online. Between 1994 and 1999, under the Digital Libraries Initiative (DLI), the federal government rewarded $68 million in research grants to help solve the challenge.[6] Among the winners were Stanford graduate students who wanted to create a better method for indexing pages on the web. Their names were Larry Page and Sergey Brin. The work they did with support from their DLI grant ended up serving as the basis for Google's search algorithm.[7]

We would not have had the Internet itself if not for government, nor would we have had some of the most important First and Second Wave companies that shaped its commercial use. Without government officials and bureaucrats—the folks so often derided in Silicon Valley—there would never have been a Silicon Valley in the first place.

GOVERNMENT AND THE THIRD WAVE

Government's role in the Third Wave will be critical in two key ways: as a regulator and as a customer. The regulatory aspect will be especially complicated as government officials weigh all kinds of new and novel challenges. Internet of Things sensor and tracking technology will give companies unprecedented access to an extraordinary level of detail about our everyday lives: not just what food you purchase but your eating habits; not just how much energy you use but how cold you like it when you sleep at night.

When a company uses education data collected daily from a student improving her reading skills, we will cheer the benefits. But what happens to that data when she graduates from high school? Does she own it? Or control it? Will a dating app one day ask her to upload it for compatibility analysis? Will they sell it? These advances are not just small steps; they are giant leaps. And they bring with them countless questions for government regulators. How should companies be allowed to use this data? What should customers know about how that data is used? And does government have a role in answering that question?

The security implications are complicated, too. There is a risk, of course, that hackers could use and exploit such data to bring a new kind of precision to fraud, identity theft, and worse. But the more frightening scenario is hackers taking control of the Internet of Things devices themselves. What happens if hackers choose to break into every pacemaker in the country instead of a government database? "If you think you've got a cybersecurity problem now, wait for a cold winter day when a hacker halfway around the world turns down the thermostat in 100,000 homes in Washington, DC," said Marc Rotenberg, the head of the Electronic Privacy Information Center.

Where does any of this fall on the regulatory spectrum? And how can government approach it in a way that balances security and privacy needs against the enormous economic potential that the Third Wave represents? Striking this balance is both critical and complicated, and anyone who professes otherwise is either naïve or being dishonest about the complexity of the task.

GOVERNMENT AS A CUSTOMER

Yet for many Third Wave companies, government won't be thought of solely as a regulatory wild card. It will also be viewed as a major potential customer. Indeed, I would expect that in the coming decades, we will see dozens of companies reach unicorn status by making products principally to sell to governments around the world.

The Environmental Protection Agency could use Internet-enabled sensors to monitor air and ocean quality with extraordinary precision. The Department of Transportation could order sensors to be embedded in every new infrastructure project, providing real-time information on everything from traffic to potholes. The Department of Defense is already deploying wearable devices for soldiers, creating an Internet-enabled front line. Cities and states, too, will surely get involved, using Third Wave integration for everything from better managing of traffic signals and energy usage to better monitoring of sewage systems and crime statistics.

The federal government is already taking steps to try to remake government services for the digital age. The White House created the US Digital Service in 2014, recruiting some of the best and brightest from the tech world and putting them to work on various challenges facing federal agencies in what *Fast Company* referred to as "Obama's stealth startup." The USDS recruits top engineers for short one- to four-year stints, putting them to work on key government projects—everything from enabling people to renew their green cards online to improving digital services for veterans. Above all, the goal is to bring the efficiency and effectiveness of the most successful Silicon Valley companies to Washington. These endeavors could be the beginning of a much-needed revamp of the federal bureaucracy and the procurement procedures it uses. The USDS could become a regular stop for rising stars in tech—much as the Peace Corps and the White House Fellows programs have been training grounds for emerging leaders.

And it might inspire some Third Wave entrepreneurs, too. The techies that the USDS is seeking to recruit know how to spot an opportunity—some of the initial hires were among the earliest employees at Facebook, Google, Amazon, and Twitter. The USDS's co-founder Todd Park was a successful serial entrepreneur before moving into government. Now they're intrigued by the idea of solving one of the biggest problems facing our nation: how to get the government functioning in a twenty-first-century context. I wouldn't be surprised if some US Digital Service veterans return to entrepreneurship after completing their stints in Washington. Having seen some of the problems with which government agencies grapple, they will be well positioned to build startups that address those challenges.

Future Third Wave entrepreneurs need to be prepared to engage with government. No one else is going to ensure that legislators understand how your company and your industry operate, where you fit into the debate, and what effects proposed policies would have. If you ignore government, a lot of governing will get done without you.

Successful engagement with government will be difficult, and it will take a willingness to listen, a foundation of respect, and a lot of patience. But it can work. It has worked. I know from experience.

HOW TO WORK WITH GOVERNMENT

The searing failure of the merger of AOL and Time Warner came down to people, relationships, and culture. We had a pretty good sense of what we should do, but we didn't have the right people, or the right culture, to capitalize on the opportunities in front of us. The lack of trust crippled the company's ability to be successful.

When I started working with and around government, I took the lessons of that experience to heart and reversed course. I focused my attention not just on coming up with ideas but on building relationships with the people who could help make them happen. I intentionally stayed out of politics. I never hosted fund-raisers or endorsed any candidate, deciding instead to remain independent and focus on building bipartisan coalitions. In 2009, this approach was put to the test.

I was asked to co-chair the newly formed National Advisory Council on Innovation & Entrepreneurship (NACIE), which consisted of more than a dozen people from various regions and sectors. NACIE ended up making a number of policy recommendations, many of which the White House embraced and put into action. Later, when President Obama launched Startup America, he asked me to chair it. We recruited a board of entrepreneurial luminaries, including Netflix's Reed Hastings, Under Armour's Kevin Plank, FedEx's Fred Smith, Dell's Michael Dell, Tory Burch, and Magic Johnson.

Soon thereafter, when he created the President's Council

on Jobs and Competitiveness, or the Jobs Council, I was asked to join that as well. I chaired the subcommittee focused on entrepreneurship, working with Sheryl Sandberg of Facebook, and John Doerr of Kleiner Perkins Caufield & Byers.

These roles gave me the chance to work with government officials in the White House and Congress. We started by engaging leaders of the business community and connecting with members of Congress from both parties to solicit their ideas. We asked McKinsey, an independent consulting firm respected by both sides, to compile a report on the various pro-innovation policies that had been proposed over the years and then rank them in terms of the positive impact they would be likely to have on spurring entrepreneurship and creating jobs.

This outreach and research enabled us to identify some policies that needed to be updated. Some of our recommendations related to updating our immigration laws so we would be better positioned to win what has become a global battle for talent. Others were focused on reducing regulations so it would be easier to start companies. We also focused on building entrepreneurship programs and infrastructure in regions outside of tech centers. But it soon became apparent that the area we should focus most on was making it easier for entrepreneurs to raise the capital they needed to start or grow businesses.

We were surprised to learn that some of the securities laws regarding raising private capital had not been updated since 1933—so they didn't take into account the reality of how venture capital worked or, for that matter, the emergence of the Internet. These longstanding regulations made it hard for entrepreneurs to raise equity capital—at a time when new banking regulations such as the Dodd-Frank Wall Street Reform and Consumer Protection Act (2010) made it harder to borrow from banks, and Sarbanes-Oxley legislation (2002) had made it harder (and more expensive) for young companies to go public. Our team worked on a handful of recommendations that could get capital flowing to more entrepreneurs, in more places, more quickly.

The resulting recommendations ranged from creating a more entrepreneur-friendly IPO on-ramp for emerging growth companies, to making it easier for entrepreneurs to seek new investors. One of the most important elements was making it possible to raise money via the Internet through crowdfunding. Companies like Kickstarter and Indiegogo had emerged to enable people to raise money for projects, and our task force wanted to make it possible for entrepreneurs to use crowdfunding to raise equity or debt capital to start or grow their companies.

All through the process, people were telling us that we were wasting our time, that our efforts would be ignored, that even if a few people paid attention, we wouldn't be able to get any legislation passed in a hyperpartisan Congress—especially in an election year. But I was convinced, as were others in the group, that we could build consensus as long as we could first build trust. So we began engaging with the key influencers at the White House and in Congress. We wanted to build support for the recommendations so that they wouldn't be ignored—and might actually get adopted.

This quiet diplomacy accelerated in the weeks leading up to the release of our report. The plan was to present the recommendations to President Obama at the January 17, 2012, meeting of his Jobs Council, but we knew that the real make-or-break work was in the lead-up to that meeting. The political climate was nastier than usual at the time, and with elections looming, we knew that if the recommendations looked as if they were coming from one side or the other, they would fail to get traction.

That the Jobs Council reported to the president—and was led by General Electric CEO Jeff Immelt—gave it some stature, but we wanted to avoid any political considerations and keep the focus on the merits of the specific policy recommendations. We arranged dozens of smaller meetings ahead of the big one, in dozens of offices, to build bipartisan support behind making the passage of pro-entrepreneurship legislation a priority—not just for the White House but for Republicans and Democrats in Congress, too.

I called Republican majority leader Eric Cantor the week before our sit-down with the president. I asked if he would meet with me the day before the Jobs Council was set to gather. He agreed. My message to him in that meeting was simple: We would issue a report the next day, outlining a series of recommendations to promote entrepreneurship and job creation.

Our effort, I explained, was resolutely bipartisan—indeed, our goal was to be nonpartisan. And I ended with a simple request: I asked him to read the recommendations before commenting on them.

The next day we unveiled our recommendations, as planned. The president was publicly supportive of the report, noting that at a time of high unemployment, both parties needed to work together to put job creation at the forefront of the nation's agenda—and that included supporting job-creating entrepreneurs.

Shortly thereafter, I met with Cantor again, to discuss the proposals. He was interested in several of them and seemed open to the idea that we might actually be able to build a bipartisan coalition to get it through Congress. It was very encouraging.

A couple of weeks later, Cantor introduced legislation called the Jumpstart Our Business Startups Act (or, as it was cleverly nicknamed, the JOBS Act). Much of the JOBS Act was based on the recommendations we made to the president. In his remarks, Cantor embraced those recommendations and urged both parties to support the legislation. The White House issued a statement of support and helped navigate passage of the legislation. I worked closely with White House advisors Gene Sperling, Jeff Zients, and Valerie Jarrett on the project. I'd worked with Gene years earlier when AOL partnered with the Clinton White House on early Internet regulations. (President Clinton embraced the promise of the Internet, and holds the distinction of having been the first president to send an email.) Jeff was a fellow DC entrepreneur and friend; we'd co-invested in a company, and our kids went to the same school. Those preexisting relationships brought trust to the table and made it possible for the participants to get comfortable with what I was trying to accomplish. I didn't know Valerie before President Obama was elected, but we had developed a strong relationship over her years in the White House as we worked together to promote entrepreneurship.

In addition to support inside Washington, we needed support beyond it. People like AngelList's Naval Ravikant and venture capitalist Kate Mitchell used the Internet to help build outside enthusiasm for the effort. With broad bipartisan support, the JOBS Act passed the House and Senate. When President Obama signed it into law at a ceremony in the Rose Garden, on April 5, 2012, I stood behind him, alongside Cantor and other JOBS Act supporters from both parties.

It was a hopeful experience. In the middle of the least productive legislative period in our history, our team managed to bring the right people together to craft a bill and get it signed into law. And it validated my view that we could build trust among otherwise warring parties. We managed to create a policy space where legislators weren't resigned to the idea that the other party was just looking to put the screws to them. The bill wasn't perfect, and no one got everything they wanted, but it provided a path forward for new business and new job creation—something everybody agreed should be a priority.

And it showed that compromise doesn't have to be anathema to politicians—something we (and they) all too often forget.

UBER: THE EXCEPTION OR THE RULE?

When I talk to people about the Third Wave and the increasing need to partner with government, someone almost always brings up Uber. After all, Uber didn't partner with government or even work with government. They employed a strategy of "ask forgiveness, not permission" (though I'm not sure they actually asked for either). And it worked. Spectacularly. Without partnerships and without consent, Uber created a platform, solicited drivers, ignored the incumbents, and emerged a near-overnight success. If it worked for Uber, why not others?

I'd say there are several reasons. First, Uber was primarily dealing with local governments—dozens, then hundreds of localities, each with different rules and regulations, different power bases, and different degrees of influence. That gave them the opportunity to employ a "divide-and-conquer" strategy, launching city by city to build enough critical mass in the marketplace. This strategy can work if it's local. But as soon as Uber's expansion took the strategy beyond the local level, they ran into trouble. There were lawsuits and regulatory challenges in nearly a dozen states. The company faced bans in Germany, the Netherlands, Brussels, and Thailand, along with parts of Australia, India, and South Africa. They had to retreat in

Spain and South Korea, where they suspended operations in response to relentless public pressure.[8] And in France, Uber executives were arrested in response to violent protests and jailed for operating an illegal taxi company. Shortly thereafter, Uber eliminated their lower-cost service there.

Still, their situation is unusual. They were facing a series of small battles, some of which they could afford to lose, as long as they could continue operating in a wide range of cities. And by the time the battles got bigger, they had the market behind them. They had the early capital to fight a multifront war—in the marketplace, in the courtrooms, and in the halls of governments throughout the world.

Additionally, Uber had the ability to provide their service, end to end, without government assistance. They didn't need the government to do anything affirmatively. They just needed it to stay out of the way. And lastly, Uber had the public on its side because of the particular regulations it was fighting. Rather than rules written to protect consumers, the rules Uber was challenging were written primarily to protect incumbent taxi companies. By arguing that they were fighting against rules that were hurting consumers, they had an easy time ginning up opposition.

This will not be the case for most Third Wave startups. A company that wants to change the way urbanites hail a car is one thing. A company that wants to revolutionize the way we lend money or deliver government services, a company that wants to connect wind power to our cities or feed the children in our schools—these kinds of disruptors will need to work with government, not as an adversary but as a partner.

THE BAY AREA VS. THE BELTWAY

As we move into the Third Wave, one of the battles I'd like to see end is the animosity that brews between Silicon Valley and Washington, DC. Some of the most famous Silicon Valley elites have adopted a hyperlibertarian view of government, convinced that it is merely an impediment to progress, an enemy of entrepreneurship, and an obstacle to innovation. One of its most famous adherents, venture capitalist Peter Thiel, sums up the world view this way: "I stand against confiscatory taxes, totalitarian collectives, and the ideology of the inevitability of the death of every individual." Whatever that means.

Here's what people like Thiel get right: Government is slow. It is frustrating. It is dysfunctional. Our legislative process is broken. Our regulatory system is outdated. And the slow pace of change in government is bad for business. But the Valley is wrong to view government as the enemy. It's wrong to measure government the same way it measures businesses. They exist in fundamentally different sectors, working with different rules, executing against different missions. The ultimate goals of government, at least in the United States and in most countries around the world, are, for the most part, noble. And when it can help, and where it can help, it can do so on a scale that no private company or nonprofit organization can contemplate.

Silicon Valley elites are also wrong to think of government officials as naïve to the needs of business. Sure, some don't get it, and some even mistrust businesses—and yes, it would be better if more of our elected officials and bureaucrats had business experience and, in particular, entrepreneurial experience. But to call them naïve is too strong. They have a different constituency—the voters—and different motivations. And they're tasked with striking the right balance between the needs of business and the needs of citizens.

Governing is a purposefully complex process, designed to be collaborative but also to include considerable restraints. Businesses don't have divided governance. A CEO can make a decision to do something and in essence compel the management team to fall in line and execute it. A president can make some executive decisions but can't make laws or authorize new spending. As a result, most of the big strategic decisions must be made collaboratively with Congress. If a board of directors and a CEO clash, the board can appoint a new CEO. Congress can't appoint a new president, and the president can't appoint a new Congress. And have you ever heard of a corporate board using a filibuster?

Where there is an intersection between business and government—or at least, where there ought to be—is on mission. It is no longer acceptable for businesses to see the world purely through the lens of profits and customers; there is also a patriotic duty to make our country stronger, our people more empowered, and the world better. That is as much a responsibility of business as it is of government.

ELEVEN

AMERICA DISRUPTED

ONE OF the pioneers of the early motion picture industry was a producer named Irving Thalberg. Thalberg produced films for MGM, hundreds of them, and he had a reputation for being an obsessive workaholic. He'd overbook his schedule, miss meetings, make important people wait for hours for an appointment. He became nearly impossible to get hold of, creating bottlenecks in his productions and frustrations among his colleagues. As legend goes, the Marx brothers once arrived for a meeting, only to hear that Thalberg would be thirty minutes late. Frustrated, they lit two cigars each and began blowing smoke under Thalberg's door.

"Is there a fire?!" Thalberg exclaimed, bursting from his office.

"No," said Groucho, "there's the Marx brothers."

Too often these days, it seems as though the only way entrepreneurs can get the government to pay attention to them is to follow Groucho's strategy: Blow smoke . . . blow a lot of smoke . . . and hope someone thinks it's fire.

For our purposes here, however, I'm not interested in blowing smoke. I've made it clear that I think that government has an essential role to play in Third Wave entrepreneurship, and that I have little patience for people who are dismissive of that role. But I am not naïve. I understand that, as important as it is for entrepreneurs to take government seriously, it's even more important for government to take entrepreneurs seriously.

Due to the magnitude of the Third Wave, we know that the benefits for American consumers can be profound. But what we don't yet know is which economy will accrue the benefits that come from Third Wave entrepreneurship. It is true, of course, that the United States has spent the better part of the century in a global leadership position. But increasingly, our incumbency has led to complacency. During the Third Wave, it may well be America that is disrupted.

This may sound overblown. But it wouldn't be the first time other countries challenged American dominance. There have been numerous occasions in our history when a great industry, born in the United States, ended up relocated elsewhere. In 2015, none of the top five automakers were American companies, and not a single American company manufactured television screens in the United States. These are industries that were born in America. We have a way, it seems, of ceding opportunities rather than seizing them. If the same holds true during the Third Wave, the most significant economic transformation of the next two decades could be the great achievement of others.

What can the United States do to prevent that future? How can we ensure that Third Wave companies choose to start here, to put down roots here, and find success here? I believe there are six areas where the government should concentrate.

Stop Confusing Startups and Small Businesses

Especially where policy is concerned, there is a meaningful difference between startups and small businesses. Both are critical to the U.S. economy, but founders who hope to build a "startup" are looking to do something fundamentally different than those looking to start a small business. In general, "startup" is a term reserved for companies that can scale quickly and that can disrupt an existing category. Startups are generally backed by venture investors who see the potential for ten or even one hundred times the return on investment. Small businesses, on the other hand, are generally funded with debt financing—a small business loan from a local bank, for example—and their aim is to grow steadily over time. They aspire to have a steady number of employees, customers, and revenues over a long period. The difference between the two is reflected both in the kinds of problems they are trying to solve and in their effect on the broader economy. Indeed, it is not small businesses but new business startups that account for nearly all of the net new job creation in the United States. The top-performing 1 percent of startups—often referred to as gazelles—are responsible for roughly 40 percent of new job creation each year.

The following chart helps illustrate the importance of start-ups to job creation.

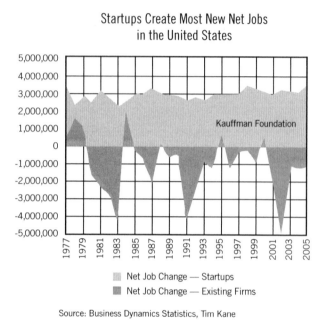

Startups Create Most New Net Jobs
in the United States

Net Job Change — Startups
Net Job Change — Existing Firms

Source: Business Dynamics Statistics, Tim Kane

The Importance of Startups (Young, High-Growth Companies) in Job Creation

When you hear most politicians talking about job creation, they tend to lump small businesses and startups together and to pursue policies that help the former more than they do the latter. It should be the opposite: If politicians want to spur job creation, their focus should be on making it easier for new *startups* to succeed.

Get in Front of the Third Wave

In 2015, journalist Darren Samuelsohn wrote an article for *Politico*, "What Washington Really Knows About the Internet of Things," in which he set out to determine "how well government was keeping up" with an industry that he predicted could end up being as much as 10 percent of the global economy.

"What I found, overall," Samuelsohn wrote,

> is that the government doesn't have any single mechanism to address the Internet of Things or the challenges it's presenting. Instead, the new networked-object technologies are covered by at least two dozen separate federal agencies—from the Food and Drug Administration to the National Highway Traffic Safety Administration, from aviation to agriculture—and more than 30 different congressional committees. Congress has written no laws or any kind of overarching national strategy specifically for the Internet of Things.

Samuelsohn's reporting is both worrying and unsurprising. Because of the size and bureaucratic nature of government, political leaders tend to act more like the fire department than the police force. Rather than patrolling for problems, they wait until something is burning.

But even once policymakers focus on it, the effort won't be easy. Because Third Wave entrepreneurship will touch so many distinct industries across every sector of the economy, the jurisdiction problems alone are overwhelming. The federal government isn't designed to regulate issues that affect so many different sectors at once. And when it tries, the result is often a patchwork of inconsistent, even contradictory, rules and a maze of confusion for the businesses trying to follow the rules.

One option would be to reduce the size of the cabinet, which now includes twenty-two people, all reporting to the president. I don't know of any CEO in America with so many direct reports. Government and business are not the same thing—not by any stretch—but this is one lesson from business that government should embrace. In 1971, President Nixon proposed reducing the cabinet to just seven departments, consolidating agencies and providing more authority to the officials who run them. Unlike other cabinet-reduction proposals, the goal here would not be to reduce the size of the federal government. Rather, it would be to reduce the inefficiency that comes with its size. There would be fewer cabinet officials, yes, but they would be meaningfully more powerful. The vice president might even act as a COO would, running a coordination effort across government and freeing up the president to be more strategic, much like a CEO.

At the same time, we should reform the Senate confirmation and vetting process, which is so long and so overreaching that it discourages some of the country's most talented people from serving, even when called upon by their president.

Of course, in Washington, something this sensible would likely be considered radical. It is not something that can be accomplished overnight. And in the meantime, businesses will keep bumping up against a deeply inefficient government, slowing the pace of innovation and allowing competitors to catch up.

As a stopgap measure, we might at least consider a temporary fix. Toward the end of 2014, an outbreak of Ebola in Africa snowballed from an isolated incident to a growing epidemic of potentially global proportions. The American public began to panic when, for the first time, Ebola made its way to the United States, infecting people who had traveled to West Africa and the medical staff who cared for them. Congress called for immediate action. President Obama recognized the growing discontent and grew increasingly concerned about the federal response. He knew the effort would have to be coordinated across several agencies. That's when my friend and colleague Ron Klain got a phone call.

Ron oversees our investment activities at Revolution and also helps provide guidance and support to The Case Foundation. He has served in many government roles, including as chief of staff to vice presidents Al Gore and Joe Biden. Ron is known for his intelligence, management skills, and problem-solving ability, and for his steady hand. That's why President Obama thought that he would be the perfect choice to become the Ebola czar. There were too many agencies working on different aspects of the crisis, and it meant that a lot of efforts weren't being coordinated. The president needed a single person reporting to him, someone to whom all of the different agencies reported—someone with the authority to work across every aspect of the federal government to clarify strategy and then execute it.

We need the exact same thing for the Third Wave. We cannot afford to have such an enormous economic opportunity get stifled by a government too slow and too fractured to respond in time. What we need is a single person within the executive branch with the authority to work across—and above—the myriad agencies, putting a clear strategy in place and managing the day-to-day execution of it across government. What we need, I believe, is a Third Wave czar.

I believe that this is only a temporary solution—that the real need is to reboot and reorganize the executive branch. Many presidents have tried, but Congress has always blocked the changes, in part out of self-interest, worried they might lose authority over an industry that supplies them with campaign contributions. More czars are a Band-Aid, not a long-term answer. In a rapidly changing world, only a government that is nimble and strategic can keep America on track.

Invest More Money in Research and Development

Thirty years from now, it's unlikely that the country will view Google (also known now as Alphabet) as our most inspiring, path-breaking, and big-thinking company. The cachet that Google now enjoys will belong to a newer, younger company. And, like Google, this new company will have made its name off technology that, in its early stages, was developed with the help of the federal government's investments in research and development—assuming, of course, that we make those necessary investments.

That's not an easy assumption to make. We should be mortified by how little we've been investing in possible breakthrough technologies. In 2015, federal investments in R&D amounted to 0.69 of a percentage point of GDP—the lowest level it's been at since the 1950s. And we've been cutting back R&D steadily over the last twenty-five years—even as federally supported R&D continues to prove its value. No wonder we now lag behind China and Germany in high-tech exports—with Singapore and South Korea following closely behind.[1]

The lack of investment has crippled programs and institutions that have been among the most critical launch pads for innovation. The National Institutes of Health, for example, has a track record of success in the field of medical research. But in 2014, the NIH's budget was 25 percent lower than it was a decade earlier. In the past, the NIH could fund one out of every three research proposals they received. By 2014, they could fund only one in six.[2]

The National Science Foundation, NASA, the Centers for Disease Control and Prevention, the Department of Defense, and the Department of Energy were among the most important government-funded R&D centers to see significant budget cuts.[3] Fifty-four percent of scientists and researchers who receive some federal funding to conduct their work were forced to lay off staff. Some began considering moving their work overseas, where more stable funding options exist.

In the field of biomedical research, federal investment has dropped every single year since 2003.[4] From 2007 to 2012, the U.S. share in total biomedical research dropped 9 percent, while the Asia-Pacific region's investment levels rose 51 percent in the same period. The new jobs and companies are following the money.[5]

Budget cuts may have been enacted out of concerns over deficits, but decreasing our investment in research and development guarantees future deficits. According to Nobel Prize–winning economist Robert Solow, we owe more than half of our GDP growth over the last fifty years to scientific breakthroughs. Yet we've been reducing our ability to undertake cutting-edge research that gives rise to disruptive technologies. In shrinking our commitments to research and development, we are decreasing our long-term economic potential and squashing our ability to create tomorrow's great innovations.

Make It Easier for Startups to Raise Money

Every single day, Americans come up with great ideas they could conceivably turn into a business. But few of them go forward with it. One of the greatest difficulties of starting a business is finding capital. If you don't have a network of contacts, it can be hard to get in front of investors. The hustle involved could turn people off from pursuing what could end up being a successful business. But it doesn't have to be this way. In the age of the Internet, connecting ideas and investors could be a much easier process—and the federal government can facilitate it.

Congress and the White House took a big step when they passed the JOBS Act, which, among other things, legalized equity-based crowdfunding. Before the JOBS Act, people could only invest in a startup if they were "accredited" by the SEC—which requires either a net worth of more than $1 million or an income of at least $200,000. And if a company had more than 500 shareholders, it had to be registered with the SEC.

These paternalistic rules had two negative effects on the economy. First, they have kept billions of investment dollars on the sideline, money that isn't being used to create companies and jobs and the value that comes with them. Second, by making it so that only the wealthy can invest in startups, the accredited investor system only exacerbates income inequality. The rich get richer, as only the accredited investors get the opportunity to invest in the startups that could become the next Facebook.

This system was modified in an important way with the JOBS Act. But after its passage in April 2012, the Securities and Exchange Commission, which was in charge of writing the rules to implement the law, took more than three years to do so. The end product was a set of rules that are still burdensome (albeit less so) for young companies. They will certainly require fine-tuning over time. I understand the need to take a careful approach to these rules. But these kinds of delays are the antithesis of the speed and nimbleness that startups require.

Once fine-tuned, the SEC rules will help, but they won't, on their own, make capital accessible for any worthy startup. There are other approaches that can increase the flow of investments into startups that Congress ought to explore. Tax incentives—like reducing tax rates on capital gains earned from certain startup investments—would drive dollars into young ventures at key stages. Any conversation about tax reform, therefore, must include these considerations. Long-term investments that can create jobs and drive growth must be encouraged.

Make It Easier to Hire Top Talent

Many consider immigration reform to be a "third rail" of American politics. Touch it and you die (or, at least, your electoral future does). But in the entrepreneurial sector, there's no such controversy. What there is instead is a recognition that we are in the middle of a global battle for talent.

There are many, many immigrants with good ideas. They come from Asia and Africa, Europe and the Middle East. According to a 2012 Kauffman Foundation study, roughly one in four tech companies established between 2006 and 2012 had at least one foreign-born founder. In Silicon Valley, nearly half did.[6] As I noted when I testified in front of the Senate Judiciary Committee advocating in favor of immigration reform, those businesses accounted for $52 billion in revenues in 2005 alone.[7]

Elon Musk, founder of Tesla, emigrated from South Africa

to Canada and then from Canada to the United States. Sergey Brin, co-founder of Google, fled the Soviet Union with his family and came to the United States as a six-year-old. As the *New York Times* put it: "Were it not for the Hebrew Immigrant Aid Society, there might be no Google."[8]

Yet even as more and more immigrants flock to the United States, the uncertainty and insecurity generated by outdated and inadequate immigration laws have hobbled our ability to compete for the best talent. The percentage of companies founded by immigrants has declined more than 16 percent since 2005,[9] and just about any startup founder can tell you what a nightmare it is to obtain a green card for a prized employee. Talented scientists and engineers are still coming to American universities to study—but all too often they are then returning home with their entrepreneurial ideas, even when they would have preferred to stay.

It's not that foreigners aren't founding companies anymore. Rather, they're being turned away from the United States, making it more likely that they'll try starting a business elsewhere, either at home or in a more hospitable country. Snapdeal was co-founded by a Wharton graduate, Kunal Bahl, but he was forced to relocate when he couldn't get a visa to stay in the United States. By 2015, Snapdeal was worth $5 billion and employed more than 5,000 people—in India.

Those jobs, and that economic growth, could have stayed in the United States if we had a more flexible immigration system. It makes no sense for us to invite students to come to the United States, train them to create economic value, and then kick them out.

America has been the most innovative and entrepreneurial nation in part because we've been an immigrant-friendly nation. As we've made it harder to come here and stay here, we've lost talent to other countries.

Most of the immigration debate within the tech industry has focused on reforming the H-1B visa program, which provides a temporary stay for foreign workers employed in specialized fields. The pool of H-1B visa holders is often a great source of employees for tech companies. But only 85,000 H-1B visas are awarded annually, with 20,000 reserved for applicants with master's degrees, while demand is much higher—U.S. Citizenship and Immigration Services received more than 172,000 petitions in 2014.[10] Increasing the number of immigrant entrepreneurs and engineers who can acquire an H-1B visa would be a boon to American businesses.

Yet, as James Surowiecki wrote in *The New Yorker* in August 2012, "In 1990, the number of employment-based permanent visas was capped at a hundred and forty thousand a year. Astonishingly, that number hasn't changed since, even though the U.S. economy is now sixty-six per cent bigger, and, with the rise of India and China, the supply of global talent has grown sharply."[11]

We need to create a Startup Visa program, one that opens the door for immigrant entrepreneurs with a proven idea to launch their startups in the United States—and, should they find success and want to stay here, gives them a route to citizenship. Reforming the H-1B visa system is important to the big tech companies, but the Startup Visa is more consequential. We've long talked about stapling a green card to graduate school diplomas—now it's time to pass legislation to do it.

The United States can remain the most innovative and entrepreneurial nation, but only if we are a magnet for the world's best and brightest. Immigration is not just a problem to solve; it's an opportunity to seize.

Write Some New Rules for a New Era

What we saw in the First and, to some extent, the Second Wave of the Internet we are seeing once again in the Third: The economy changes far faster than the rules governing it. The system we have in place to regulate business is stuck on twentieth-century notions of how the American economy works—some of which no longer make sense.

Companies such as Uber and Instacart (an on-demand grocery delivery service), which rely on individuals who work on a project-to-project basis, are leading us to rethink ideas about employment and what it means to be a worker. These companies give people the flexibility to work their own hours as they see fit, and the compensation to make a good income for those hours. But this new approach is not without some problems—for example, some workers are concerned that they don't have protections against losing their contractor status for undue cause. Specifically, as the "uberization" of more and more industries takes hold, how will the middle class earn paid sick leave, vacation days, and unemployment insurance and contribute to their retirement plans?

A primary reason why these issues are emerging is that our legal system's view of employment wasn't designed for the freelance economy. Rather, it was written into New Deal legislation, which divided workers into two categories: full employees and independent contractors. That worked for decades, but it doesn't work anymore. A large part of the labor force of these startups is now composed of people who work only a few hours a week.

There is a happy medium that can exist between full employment status, which usually confers benefits and stability to employees, and contractor status, which provides flexibility and mobility. Preserving the rights of workers and enabling economic growth do not have to be mutually exclusive aims— but they will be if we stick to old definitions of employment. As Senator Mark Warner put it in the *Washington Post*, "Instead of trying to make the new economy look more like the old, Washington should encourage these innovations and work to create more opportunities and upward economic mobility for everybody." It's up to the government to take an active role in establishing a fair compromise that allows us to do just that. There's a tremendous upside in getting this right—not just for the companies in question but for middle- and low-income workers. If the government creates a new employment designation that both allows for this sort of on-demand work structure and provides basic worker protections, it could open a new path to socioeconomic mobility.

That's not to say that climbing the socioeconomic ladder will become easy. But it's not as if the people who will be in a position to benefit from the freelance economy have it easy now. Undereducated workers today have few options to move up. By and large, it's difficult for such workers to find the time or resources to dedicate to furthering their education. The people who manage to do so while working low-wage jobs are practically superhuman. But that shouldn't be the requirement for living a good life in America.

TIME IS NOT ON OUR SIDE

Other countries don't have the same preoccupations we do. They've watched America grow and prosper and have studied our methods, and now they are working to do the same for themselves. All around the world, nations are working to replicate the conditions necessary for a vibrant entrepreneurial environment. They're encouraging entrepreneurship, making it easier to start and run businesses, increasing access to capital, and creating the support networks needed to better position their citizen entrepreneurs—and those they can attract to their shores—for success.

In 2013, Canada launched its Start-Up Visa Program, offering permanent residence to entrepreneurs willing to move to Canada and start a business or relocate their current one. As Employment Minister Jason Kenney put it, "We're seeking very deliberately to benefit from the dysfunctional American immigration system. I make no bones about it."[12] In Chile, the government launched a flagship seed accelerator program called Start-Up Chile in 2010. The goal was to create Chile's own "mini Silicon Valley," which could provide a boost to an economy that was already one of Latin America's fastest growing. Europe, too, is waking up and embracing the entrepreneurship imperative. Cities such as London, Helsinki, Stockholm, and Berlin are becoming thriving startup communities. London leapfrogged San Francisco and New York as the world's top city for crowdfunding in 2013. And the British government is trying to modify their regulatory environment to position the UK as the fintech capital of the world.

South Korea, meanwhile, is working to rid the stigma associated with failure—a fear that every entrepreneurial nation must conquer—through investing $2.9 billion in startups. And China wants to grow its skilled worker pool to over 180 million by the end of the decade.[13] In doing so, they hope to reverse the trend in which Chinese citizens leave the country to study at premier universities and end up contributing to other economies—including ours.

We also see emerging startup sectors in the Middle East and Africa—creating a more stable world and new competitors, all at once. Israel is widely praised as a preeminent "startup nation" and is making huge investments in basic technology.

We've seen the creation of venture capital funds in the West Bank to fund entrepreneurs who can create jobs, opportunity, and hope in the region. (I'm proud to note that The Case Foundation was a catalyst for the creation of one such fund when my wife, Jean, co-chaired the U.S.-Palestinian Partnership for President George W. Bush.)

Africa is on the move, with Nigeria and Kenya in particular emerging as hotbeds of entrepreneurial innovation. And we're even seeing an entrepreneurial culture break out in Cuba. After a half century of being held back by socialism, Cubans are preparing for an innovation revolution. Small businesses, long banned, are now permitted, and some of those small businesses may, over time, become big businesses.

These regions and nations are moving forward at a time when America is trending sideways in certain areas and moving backward in others. And the tools that have long been available to entrepreneurs in America are increasingly available to entrepreneurs all over the world.

It seems everywhere you look in the world—from Australia[14] to Zambia[15]—governments are working with the private sector to optimize a startup-friendly environment. Admittedly, these are not imminent threats. Lagos isn't going to leapfrog Silicon Valley in the next six months, or even the next six years. Nor is Santiago, São Paulo, or Seoul. But that doesn't mean we should be content with where we stand today. And it certainly doesn't mean that we shouldn't seek to be better. Losing our entrepreneurial edge is not just about how we are doing in comparison to other countries. It's how we are doing in comparison to our own potential.

The American economy is an entrepreneurial ecosystem. To get growth, we need to support growth. We need new ideas coming out of R&D labs, which entrepreneurs can then adapt for commercialization, knowing they have the runway they need to scale and succeed. And then we need to do it all over again. That's what will create the jobs and the economic activity that will maintain our position on the point of the spear. But if any of those groups fails to make a contribution, the system breaks down. Already, the government's failure to support our entrepreneurial community properly is costing us countless jobs and economic growth.

America led in the First Wave, and again in the Second Wave. We can—and should—lead in the Third Wave. If we take the right actions and do it quickly, a bright future will be assured. If we fail to, the world will no longer look to us as a source of radical innovation. Instead, we'll end up playing catch-up, attempting to emulate the creations of other nations rather than introducing the ideas that others try to copy.

It won't mean the end of America. But likely it will mean the end of American leadership. And that's a future we all must work to avoid.

TWELVE

RIDE THE WAVE

I N JUNE 1983, I was at a crossroads. I was twenty-four years old and had spent a year working for Pizza Hut. And while I had a good time traveling the country and stuffing myself, the job was starting to get old. That summer I made a pros and cons list. I wrote down various career options—going to an established company, a startup, or a consulting firm—and ticked through the benefits and drawbacks of each possible move.

First on my list were established tech companies such as Apple and Atari. Marketing positions at those companies would have provided the tech on-ramp I was seeking, but with big companies come internal politics and red tape. There were some pros to those jobs but also a whole lot of cons.

When considering the possibility of joining a marketing consulting firm in San Francisco, I noted that while it would be fun to work in Silicon Valley, I had three concerns: "stuffy, tough sell, don't like consulting." So that was a pass, too.

Finally, there was CVC, the startup I ended up choosing. I saw a lot of upside to going there: an exciting idea, promising technology, a chance to make a big impact in a growing market—and, best of all, the opportunity to work alongside and learn from entrepreneur Bill von Meister. I listed only one downside: "future uncertain."

Everything about that CVC job was up in the air, from my future role in the company to the future of the company itself. Of course, you know how the story ends, but at the time this was a big concern. In a way, though, that uncertainty was as much a pro as it was a con. Sure, an uncertain future meant I could be out on the streets looking for a job in a few months' time. But it also meant a chance to make my own destiny. A chance, as it turned out, to play a role in making the Internet a part of everyday life.

I'm often reminded of the famous newspaper ad Ernest Shackleton is said to have placed before his 1914 attempt to explore Antarctica: "Men wanted for hazardous journey. Small wages. Bitter cold. Long months of complete darkness. Constant danger. Safe return doubtful. Honor and recognition in case of success."[1] That's the beauty of entrepreneurship, and that's what drew me to CVC.

The bottom line is that when I was twenty-four, I had no idea where my own "hazardous journey" would lead me. I didn't know whether my stock options would even be worth the paper they were printed on. All I knew was that in the uncertainty lay immense challenges—and enormous opportunities. There was a boundless electronic frontier to explore, an online Antarctica filled with peril and possibility. And I knew that I needed to be a part of charting that uncertain future.

When I think about what the world will look like thirty years from now and try to anticipate what problems we need to solve—to say nothing of the problems we face now—I see another uncertain future. But I also believe that, as in my case, this uncertainty isn't a disadvantage. Once again, we've got a pro masquerading as a con. Once again, we have the opportunity—and, I believe, the obligation—to set a new course. Now we just have to think about what all of us—entrepreneurs, business leaders, government officials, everyday Americans with good ideas—can and must do to make sure we arrive there.

MY KEY TAKEAWAYS

If you've decided to skim this book or skip to the end, I won't take offense as long as you stop here. These are the things you're going to need to remember, whether you're a budding entrepreneur, a corporate executive, or a casual reader.

The Third Wave of the Internet is coming, the moment where the Internet transforms from something we interact with to something that interacts with everything around us. It will mean the rise of the Internet of Everything, where everything we do will be enabled by an Internet connection, much in the way it's already enabled by electricity. This process will lead to the transformation of some of the industries that are vital to our daily lives, which will make the barriers to success higher, and the need to form partnerships much more central, as a way of building credibility, opening doors, and getting past industry gatekeepers. One such partner will likely be the government, which has an interest in regulating the industries most affected by the Third Wave. Don't confuse your views of government with the role of government, which can be either an impediment to progress or a driver of it, and which cannot be ignored. Much Third Wave innovation will come from impact entrepreneurs focused on building "profit plus purpose" companies that have a measurable impact in the world. And this innovation will be geographically dispersed, as the rest of the country (and the world) rises up to complement the innovation now occurring largely in a few places, such as Silicon Valley. The challenges in the Third Wave will be vexing, and as Thomas Edison reminds us, "Vision without execution is hallucination." But if we rally together, and execute with precision, we can remain the world's most innovative and entrepreneurial nation.

So that's my thesis, in a nutshell. Think of it as the CliffsNotes—or *BuzzFeed*—guide to the Third Wave. But before closing, I want to share a few parting thoughts.

A MESSAGE TO ENTREPRENEURS

In practically every disaster movie—be it *Independence Day* or *World War Z* or *Godzilla*—there comes a moment when a character looks at the protagonist and says something to the effect of "The fate of the planet is in your hands." Our hero always gulps, looks terrified, and then blasts off to blow up the asteroid or defeat the rampaging aliens before they take out New York City.

Fortunately, there is no asteroid bearing down on Earth (that we know of). But if we're being honest, here in the second decade of the twenty-first century, we're facing our fair share of serious obstacles.

To those who consider themselves entrepreneurs: Our country—and the world—depends on you. Our future is going to rise and fall with the dreamers and doers, the builders of new technologies and the breakers of old orthodoxies.

So let us set our ambitions high. Let us worry a little less about our net worth and a little more about our net impact. I disagree with the anonymous Apple executive who claimed, in a 2013 *New Yorker* article, "We don't have an obligation to solve America's problems. Our only obligation is making the best product possible."[2] Entrepreneurs *do* have a responsibility to do more than make cool gadgets and popular apps, not because those products aren't valuable but because, at a time when smart solutions are at a premium, our most valuable resource—the endlessly firing neurons in the brains of our t people—ought to be directed at our biggest chal-

.

ᴜur healthcare system is really a *sick* care system—and a system that produces mediocre outcomes at high cost and with low levels of convenience. Innovative tech and genomics startups are poised to reverse that trend, and hold out the potential that we can focus more on wellness, improve outcomes, reduce costs, and boost convenience.

Then there are educational innovations that harness the power of the Internet to expand access to learning. Emerging edtech startups have the potential to democratize learning, personalize it for each student, and offer more teaching, with greater convenience, at lower cost. That isn't untethered futurism; it's happening now, in a growing number of schools, and we need to take the best approaches and scale them nationally.

Financial services are being disrupted in unprecedented ways, as new lending and investing platforms are emerging from outside the traditional banking system. Transportation is being reimagined, as self-driving cars and perhaps even a supersonic Hyperloop begin to make the shift from science fiction to reality. Everything from energy to insurance, from agriculture to manufacturing, is transforming. In the Third Wave, there will be opportunities to innovate in every sector, touching every aspect of our lives. So think about how you can attack these old, often intractable problems in new ways.

And remember this: The Internet of Everything will affect

every aspect of our lives, in increasingly seamless ways. Use this tool to your advantage.

Remember that companies will be addressing core societal needs and broad-scale change—and that many will be focused on impact and purpose, not just profit.

Remember that entrepreneurship will be regionalizing and globalizing, so you can start this adventure in your own backyard.

Remember that entrepreneurs as "soloists" will be replaced by orchestras playing a stronger, more credible tune. That if you want to go far in the Third Wave, you must go together.

Remember that the sectors that matter to people are regulated by the government, and so the great leaps of the Third Wave will require a respect for policy.

And remember, finally, that the Third Wave will happen in revolutionary, but also evolutionary, ways—more slowly than you may like, but more profoundly than you can imagine.

Whatever you choose, I hope you will pursue the disruptive ideas that will create the most value—not just for your company but for your country and the world. Because that old truism is right: The Stone Age didn't end because we ran out of stone. It ended because we invented something better.

A MESSAGE TO CORPORATE AMERICA

To corporate leaders, it's time to develop a perpetual sense of paranoia and curiosity. It's time to both fear the future and seize its promise, to restlessly drive to master it, no matter what it holds. Regardless of where you and your company stand at the end of today, you can always wake up tomorrow to find that things have changed drastically. You jeopardize your position if you don't strive to anticipate *how* it will change.

Keep your finger on the pulse of technology, and consider what its beat might mean for your business. Take stock of trends. Resist the temptation to dismiss up-and-coming technologies.

Empower your team to ask questions and, where no answers exist, to create new ones. Give them the space to innovate and experiment. Take more "shots on goal." Allow more crazy ideas to bubble up, because the very best ideas often sound ridiculous when first proposed. Surely, executives at Marriott and Hilton would have thought that the idea of renting an air mattress or a room in an apartment was insane. But in 2015, seven years after starting, Airbnb was valued at $25 billion, making it worth more than either of the hospitality powerhouses, both of which have been around for more than half a century. And it's not just about relative valuations: it's also about sudden shifts in market dynamics. As Senator Marco Rubio has pointed out, Airbnb is now the largest hospitality provider, yet they don't own a single hotel. Similarly, Uber is the largest transportation company, though they don't own a single vehicle. And neither company existed just a decade ago.

Remember that disruption has broadened. Your competitors won't just emerge from the low end of your industry.

Increasingly, they'll come from other industries, too. Apple wasn't in the music business, nor was Google in the mobile phone business—until suddenly they were. So build a network in and around your company—and look for opportunity in every direction.

The future belongs to those who endeavor to create it. That's why we go into business—because we have a vision for the future that we want to see through. So don't let temporary successes permanently blind your future ambitions.

You have the resources—human, capital, and otherwise— to take on ambitious projects. And so you must decide—is it better to use those resources to resist change or to drive it?

And remember this: In the Third Wave, partnerships will become more important. You'll have more opportunities in the next decade than you did in the past decade. So don't just play defense, play offense. Don't just defend, attack. But don't go it alone. As Helen Keller said, "Alone we can do so little. Together we can do so much."

A MESSAGE TO GOVERNMENT

If entrepreneurs have a responsibility to devote their talents to making a lasting, positive impact on society, then government has an equally important obligation to encourage entrepreneurship and smooth the way for new ideas to take off. Government plays a pivotal role in enabling successful startups.

It's a sentiment we hear expressed repeatedly, on both sides of the aisle. But while our politicians love to tell us how important it is to encourage entrepreneurship, talk is often cheap. If our elected officials truly want to support the next Jobs or Zuckerberg or Musk, they must replace those platitudes with policies.

We must reduce the regulatory burdens on entrepreneurs while forging a new path forward for new industries. We must support the rise-of-the-rest regions, so America's innovation economy will be more broadly dispersed. We must make the playing field level, so every entrepreneur with a good idea has a shot at raising capital. We must reimagine—and restructure—government to be responsive in the Third Wave. And we must reform our immigration system so we can win the global battle for talent. We know what we need to do—now we just need to come together, in a bipartisan fashion, to position the United States to remain the most innovative and entrepreneurial nation.

A MESSAGE TO ALL SIDES

That will only happen if all sides—programmers and policymakers, entrepreneurs and elected officials—get over their various perceived slights and incompatibilities and work together. During the Cold War, the White House and the Kremlin had that famous "red phone" to make sure they could reach each other in case of any serious misunderstandings. Here in the twenty-first century, we should have a similar hotline, a "red iPhone" between Washington and Silicon Valley. And that line should always be open.

It's clear to me that this relationship has a big disconnect that we need to bridge. We need engineers to understand Congress, and Congress to understand entrepreneurs. And both need to be better, not just at listening to one another, but at taking action to support each other, too.

Above all, we need to remember that, fundamentally, business and government want the same thing: to add value to people's lives. Our society has been strengthened by both Social Security and cybersecurity, by the Air Force and by Airbnb. And whether it's through an ingenious product or a life-changing social program, a disruptive innovation or a constructive piece of legislation, CEOs and members of Congress alike aim to make our lives safer, easier, happier, and more productive. We should remember that there's more that unites us than divides us. After all, what is the United States if not the most successful startup in the history of the world?

This relationship will not be "frictionless," to use a favorite Silicon Valley buzzword. We're not going to get every tedious regulation off the books or reach a perfect consensus on when and how companies should share their customers' private data with intelligence agencies. But as technology increasingly intersects with government—from the need for a functional HealthCare.gov website to the challenging questions raised by growing government surveillance—a strong and productive relationship between entrepreneurs and government is a necessity.

ely, for both sides to add to this country—to add services, to add value—we need to stop subtracting from one another's work. The best answers to our problems won't originate in the Oval Office or in a garage in Palo Alto. They'll arise, as so many of our most innovative ideas have, from connections between different people in different places drawing on a wealth of different perspectives.

A MESSAGE TO YOU

So now I come to you. If you're reading this book, it's clear that you care about the future of entrepreneurship and the potential of the Third Wave. Ideas excite you, the bigger the better. Maybe you have one yourself. But if you're still reading this book, perhaps I haven't yet given you a good enough reason to put it down and turn that idea into a reality. So if you're thinking about taking the leap, let me give you a little nudge.

When I was graduating from college and not yet sure what I was going to do, I applied to a couple of business schools. They asked for a personal statement, so I wrote:

> I firmly believe that technological advances in communication are on the verge of significantly altering our way of life. Innovations in telecommunications (especially two-way cable systems) will result in our television sets becoming an information lifeline, newspaper, computer, school, referendum machine, and catalog.

Clearly, this will have a drastic effect on advertising, as will changes in the number, ages, and working habits of the U.S. population. The new technologies will fragment the home audience and allow advertisers and agencies to escape from the rigidity of commercial formats and develop communications forms appropriate to individual advertisers and their target audiences. More sophisticated testing techniques in persuasion and effectiveness measurements will have to be developed to take advantage of the ability advertisers will have to isolate specific groups of customers.

More importantly, the industry must develop executives who have an understanding of the people who live in an electronic society and what motivates them, and the ability to *anticipate* problems that need to be solved.

I thought all of that made a lot of sense when I wrote and submitted my applications back in 1980. And yet every business school to which I applied rejected me.

But the trends I wrote about nearly four decades ago proved to be pretty accurate. Today, technological advances in communication aren't "on the verge" of altering our way of life—they've already transformed it. The Internet hasn't just had "a drastic effect" on advertising—it has revolutionized how businesses interact with consumers. And it's more essential than ever that each and every industry develop executives who understand the people who live in an electronic society and anticipate the problems they'll need solved.

And that's where you come in. It was my great fortune to help get America online. It's up to you to get America—and the world—on track, to lead the Third Wave and beyond. To help us ride the bleeding edge of the next big thing. To be honest, I'm a little envious. You won't find any experience more gratifying or exhilarating—especially now, as the Third Wave creates the possibility for such meaningful change.

This moment should speak to the innovator inside you. The one who refuses to accept the world as it is. It should invoke an urge to explore, to question, to push boundaries. It's an urge I encourage you to heed, whether you're a serial entrepreneur or a corporate executive debating whether to take the plunge.

There will be headaches and heartaches—I guarantee it. The naysayers will be out in full force. But these are the people who saw the first automobiles, in 1896, and jeered, "Get a horse!"[3] They're the ones who didn't know how to pronounce the word "Internet" and never thought they'd need to. Your job—your only job—is to stay relentlessly focused on that voice in your head that tells you, "It can be done." Or, as Nelson Mandela said in another context, "It always seems impossible until it's done."

Yes, the future is uncertain—and that's what makes it so exciting. And yes, it will be hard—which is why it's important to remember what Teddy Roosevelt said a century ago:

> It is not the critic who counts. . . . The credit belongs to the man who is actually in the arena, whose face is marred by dust and sweat and blood; who strives val-

iantly; who errs, who comes short again and again,
cause there is no effort without error and shortcomin
but who does actually strive to do the deeds; who knows
great enthusiasms, the great devotions; who spends himself in a worthy cause; who at the best knows in the end
the triumph of high achievement, and who at the worst,
if he fails, at least fails while daring greatly, so that his
place shall never be with those cold and timid souls who
neither know victory nor defeat.

So put down this book. Pick up your smartphone, your
notepad—your blowtorch, if you're feeling ambitious. Take
action. Be fearless. You may stumble, but get back up. Keep
going. Keep tinkering, perhaps late at night, after the children
are in bed. Build something that makes you proud—but not
satisfied enough to stop dreaming about what comes next.
Enter the arena. Topple an empire and build your own from
the ground up.

The world is waiting. Are you?

ACKNOWLEDGMENTS

THIS IS my first book. F. Scott Fitzgerald once said, "You don't write because you want to say something, you write because you have something to say." I've resisted the various calls over the years to write a history of AOL or the Internet, because I've always been more interested in the future than in the past. The impetus to finally set pen to paper was the recognition that the Internet's Third Wave will likely have a lot of similarities to the First Wave. Once I realized that the future will be informed by the past, I jumped into the project with vigor.

Having waited two decades to write a book, I felt the pressure was on to make it the best I could. I knew I couldn't get very far on my own, so I assembled a crack team to take my ideas and give them flight.

It started with Walter Isaacson. I've known Walter for more than twenty years, and we first kicked around the idea of writing a book together six years ago when we were on a flight together. Shortly thereafter he was approached by Steve Jobs to write an authorized biography, and then he went on to pen *The Innovators*, his history of the digital revolution. When I told Walter I had decided to write *The Third Wave*, he immediately offered to help. Walter was an early reader of my initial draft, and his comments were invaluable. He also offered to write the foreword, for which I am grateful.

I've always believed in the wisdom of crowds, so I asked dozens of friends to read various iterations of this book. This "crowdsourced" book is better because of their insights. Some spent countless hours helping me through this journalistic journey, and their detailed, candid comments were incredibly helpful. My longtime friend (and former AOL board member) Colin Powell told me to include more stories to bring the book to life ("More cowbell," he urged). Tom Tierney gave me valuable organizational suggestions, helping improve the structure immeasurably (perhaps not surprising, given that he was formerly CEO of Bain). Ted Leonsis, a great friend and my partner of more than two decades at both AOL and now at Revolution, offered great insights on our many shared experiences. David Petraeus administered some tough love ("Ask a soldier for his opinion and you'll get just that," he told me, after reading my first draft). Brad Feld brought an entrepreneurial perspective, having co-founded Techstars (and as the author of a half-dozen books on startups); he helped me frame a call to arms for a new era of entrepreneurs. The always diligent Don Graham sent me suggestions on almost every page, mustering a lifetime of business and editorial experience with his insights. Ross Baird has joined me on every rise-of-the-rest bus tour, and provided thoughtful insights on regional and inclusive entrepreneurship. Former entrepreneur and now congressman John Delaney provided unique perspectives on rebooting government to unleash innovation, as only somebody who has bridged both worlds could. So did Todd

Park, a serial entrepreneur who went on to serve as White House chief technology officer, and Frank Raines, a longtime colleague who managed the Office of Management and Budget the last time the nation balanced its budget. Jon Huntsman brought a global perspective, and his comments (sent, appropriately, while he was traveling in the Middle East) reminded me that many nations have figured out that the "secret sauce" that has propelled America to greatness is innovation and entrepreneurship. Dominic Barton, the global managing director of McKinsey & Company, provided invaluable strategic perspectives, especially about the challenges Fortune 500 companies face in the world of disruption. And Norm Augustine, the former CEO of Lockheed Martin, shared critical insights about the need to bridge the worlds of business and government.

Those were just a few of the dozens of people I consulted as I sought to refine and sharpen this book. I'm also grateful for the generous and constructive feedback I received from friends such as David Agus, John Bridgeland, Warren Buffett, Steve Clemons, Tom Davidson, Jiggs Davis, Doug Holladay, Jeff Immelt, Michael Lynton, John McCarter, Lenny Mendonca, Kristin Groos Richmond, David Rubenstein, Sheryl Sandberg, Marc Seriff, Jim Shelton, Peter Sims, David Skorton, Michael Smith, Alan Spoon, Kirsten Saenz Tobey, and Sheel Tyle, as well as the many colleagues at Revolution and The Case Foundation who shared their insights, including Philippe Bourguignon, Erich Broksas, Donn Davis, David Golden, Sheila Herrling, Scott Hilleboe, Evan Morgan, Brian Sasscer, Tige Savage, and Clara Sieg.

I couldn't have written this book without the considerable help of the superb team we assembled, led by the immensely capable Ron Klain. This effort benefited greatly from the guidance and steady hand of Bob Barnett. And much of the heavy lifting was done by Dylan Loewe and the team at West Wing Writers. They combed through the hundreds of speeches I've delivered and interviews I've done over the years, supplemented that with research to flesh out key points, and played a crucial role in helping me organize and write the book. Allie Burns, Marissa Hopkins Secreto, Herbie Ziskend, and Andria Kolesnikoff were invaluable members of the core team—endeavoring to make this an interesting book and to maximize the likelihood of its reaching a wide audience.

Simon & Schuster played an essential role as well. I had the opportunity to meet with a number of publishers to discuss the book, but instantly connected with Jon Karp and Ben Loehnen, and benefited throughout the process from their insights and encouragement.

Over the past decade I've had the opportunity to meet with thousands of entrepreneurs. I've been inspired by their stories and impressed by their aspirations. My investment firm, Revolution, has had the great privilege of backing nearly one hundred companies since our launch a decade ago. My thanks go to the entrepreneurs who picked us to be their partner; our fellow investors who helped us help the entrepreneurs turn their dreams into great companies; to the thousands and thousands of employees who power those companies every day; and to the tens of millions of consumers who have bought their products or used their services. We've long said we invest in people and ideas that can change the world, and we're humbled by the opportunity to make an impact, both at Revolution and at The Case Foundation.

I mentioned at the outset that I was inspired by reading Alvin Toffler's *The Third Wave* when I was in college in 1980—indeed, so inspired that I decided to pay homage by using the same title for this "2.0" version. I can only dream that some young people reading this book might be similarly inspired.

Thanks are, of course, also in order to my family. I first met my wife, Jean, when she interviewed for a job at AOL in 1988. I'm glad we convinced her to leave GE to join our fledgling startup, as she played a central role in AOL's rise—and in my life. She was also my closest and most insightful advisor throughout the book process, and has brilliantly led The Case Foundation since its founding nearly two decades ago. I'm appreciative of my parents, Dan and Carol Case, who stood by me through the various ups and downs, and my siblings Carin and Jeff—and my late brother, Dan, who played a major role in my entrepreneurial rise (and also his wife, Stacey, who stepped up to fill the resulting void). I'm thankful for my three kids, Everett, Annie, and Katie, as well as my two stepdaughters, Nikki and Katie—and I'm grateful they are on terrific trajectories now as adults (#SoProud). I'm also indebted to my ex-wife, Joanne Barker; she supported me in the early AOL years and was pivotal in raising great (and grounded) kids.

I wouldn't have a story to write if it hadn't been for the team that brought AOL to life. I will always be indebted to my co-founders, Jim Kimsey and Marc Seriff, and the dozens of pioneers who stuck with us in those difficult first years—as well as the hundreds, and then thousands, of people who joined our team as AOL expanded. When we started up in 1985, only 3 percent of American households were online, and most people didn't see the need to ever get online. By the time I stepped down as CEO in 2000 (to facilitate the merger with Time Warner), the Internet had come of age, and nearly half of all U.S. Internet traffic flowed through AOL. None of that would have been possible without our tireless team. I learned firsthand that entrepreneurship is a team sport, and we certainly had the dream team.

I also want to thank the tens of millions of people who believed in AOL and joined us as we sought to get America online. Thanks for giving those AOL free trial discs a try! We would never have succeeded without your support. Your belief in us made this story possible.

Lastly, I want to thank the next generation of entrepreneurs, the ones who are tinkering with their ideas at their desks or in their garages. They give me hope that *The Third Wave* will usher in an exciting new era of innovation—and that, through their efforts, America can in fact remain the most entrepreneurial nation in the world.

NOTES

TWO **GETTING AMERICA ONLINE**

1. See http://ir.timewarner.com/phoenix.zhtml?c=70972&p=irol
   -faq. AOL went public March 19, 1992.

2. http://www.cbsnews.com/news/the-day-america-online-went
   -offline-in-1996/

THREE **THE THIRD WAVE**

1. http://www.mckinsey.com/~/media/mckinsey/dotcom/insights
   /business%20technology/unlocking%20the%20potential%
   20of%20the%20internet%20of%20things/unlocking_the_
   potential_of_the_internet_of_things_executive_summary.ashx

FIVE **THE THREE P'S**

1. http://techcrunch.com/2011/09/14/elon-musk-starting-a
   -company-is-like-staring-into-the-face-of-death/

SEVEN **THE RISE OF THE REST**

1. http://americanunderground.com/1-billion-6-exits-24-mos
   -durham-nc/

2. http://www.kauffman.org/what-we-do/resources/entrepreneurship
   -policy-digest/the-importance-of-young-firms-for-economic
   -growth

3. http://www.datacenterresearch.org/reports_analysis/economic
   -timeline/

4. http://www.ncdc.noaa.gov/extremeevents/specialreports /Hurricane-Katrina.pdf

5. Ibid.

6. http://www.nola.com/futureofneworleans/2015/07/future_new _orleans_entrepreneu.html

7. http://bits.blogs.nytimes.com/2015/06/28/new-diversity-reports-show-the-same-old-results/?_r=0

8. http://www.si.edu/Exhibitions/Details/Places-of-Invention-4626

NINE A MATTER OF TRUST

1. http://abcnews.go.com/Business/Decade/aol-buys-time-warner-162-billion/story?id=9279138

2. http://archive.wired.com/wired/archive/7.10/aoldata.html

3. http://w3.nexis.com/new/docview/getDocForCuiReq?oc =00240&lni=4S33-6N40-TX4X-W0GM&perma=true&csi =8399&secondRedirectIndicator=true

4. http://w3.nexis.com/new/docview/getDocForCuiReq?oc =00240&lni=3T4V-0260-008R-F2RV&perma=true&csi =8399&secondRedirectIndicator=true

5. http://money.cnn.com/2000/01/10/deals/aol_warner/

6. http://www.timewarner.com/newsroom/press-releases/2000 /01/10/america-online-and-time-warner-will-merge-to-create-world-s-first

7. http://www.cnet.com/news/nasdaq-5000-ten-years-after-the-dot-com-peak/

8. From http://papers.ssrn.com/sol3/papers.cfm?abstract_id= 776228, cited to Nina Munk's book *Fools Rush In*. Apparently it's on page 277 of the edition published in 2004.

TEN **THE VISIBLE HAND**

1.   http://nuclearfutures.princeton.edu/courses/wws353/

2.   Ibid.

3.   http://www.nrl.navy.mil/accomplishments/systems/radar/

4.   https://www.asis.org/Bulletin/Oct-99/fox.html

5.   http://www.faseb.org/portals/2/pdfs/opa/2008/nih_research
     _benefits.pdf

6.   https://www.asis.org/Bulletin/Oct-99/fox.html

7.   https://www.nsf.gov/discoveries/disc_summ.jsp?cntn_id
     =100660

8.   http://www.businessinsider.com/heres-everywhere-uber-is
     -banned-around-the-world-2015-4

ELEVEN **AMERICA DISRUPTED**

1.   http://www.politico.com/agenda/story/2015/06/kevin-ashton
     -internet-of-things-in-the-us-000102

2.   http://www.usatoday.com/story/news/nation/2014/04/23/nih
     -budget-cuts/8056113/

3.   http://www.washingtonpost.com/national/health-science/budget
     -sequester-squeezes-scientists/2013/09/24/a88f3686-1caa-11e3
     -82ef-a059e54c49d0_story.html

4.   Ibid.

5.   http://www.huffingtonpost.com/2014/01/03/science
     -sequestration_n_4536209.html

6.   http://www.washingtonpost.com/wp-dyn/content/article/2007
     /01/03/AR2007010301402.html

7.   http://www.judiciary.senate.gov/imo/media/doc/2-13-13
     CaseTestimony.pdf

8.   http://www.nytimes.com/2009/10/25/us/25donate.html

9. http://www.kauffman.org/newsroom/2012/11/immigrant
   -entrepreneurship-has-stalled-for-the-first-time-in-decades
   -kauffman-foundation-study-shows

10. http://articles.economictimes.indiatimes.com/2014-04-11/news
    /49058680_1_advanced-degree-exemption-uscis-h-1b-petitions

11. http://www.newyorker.com/magazine/2012/08/27/the-track
    -star-economy

12. http://www.leaderpost.com/business/immigration+loss+Canada
    +gain/10127038/story.html

13. http://www.nytimes.com/roomfordebate/2013/01/21/the-effects
    -of-chinas-push-for-education/educated-workers-are-good-for
    -china-and-the-rest-of-the-world

14. http://ventureburn.com/2014/02/russias-entrepreneurial
    -landscape-according-to-ernst-young-ew/

15. http://www.economist.com/node/21548263

TWELVE **RIDE THE WAVE**

1. http://main.wgbh.org/imax/shackleton/sirernest.html

2. http://www.newyorker.com/magazine/2013/05/27/change-the
   -world

3. http://books.google.com/books?id=qNVrfoSubmIC&printsec
   =frontcover&dq=why+the+west+rules+for+now&hl=en&sa
   =X&ei=6jl-VO-9NpGSyAS034HgBA&ved=0CB4Q6wEwAA#v=
   onepage&q=%22Get%20a%20horse%22&f=false

INDEX

Adelson, Merv, xii
Aetna, 140
Africa, 161, 176, 182, 183
  Ebola outbreak (2014), 170–71
  proverb, 69
agriculture industry, 51, 81–82, 84, 95
Airbnb, 192
Allen, Paul, 60–62, 64, 65
Amazon, 3, 39, 85, 103, 132, 154
American Tobacco, 91
Andreessen, Marc, 115
AngelList, 160
AOL (America Online), xiii, xiv, 2
  accounting scandal (2002), 137–38
  acquisitions, 36, 114–17
  broadband and web threats, xii,
    118
  Case as CEO, 33–34, 38, 39–41,
    56–67, 114–25
  CDs, 7
  Commodore and, 22–23, 73
  competitors, 56–67, 73, 139
  CompuServe buyout offer, 59–60
  credibility challenge, 72–75
  culture of, 104
  diversifying the business, 115–17
  as dominant Internet provider,
    40–41, 67, 137
  first service (1985), xiii
  growth, 37–38, 40, 114
  headquarters, 31, 38, 64, 104–5,
    117
  IBM Promenade and, 57–58, 73

importance of, 38–39
Instant Messenger, 3, 39, 116, 136
investors in, 33, 34, 66, 104
IPO, 34–36, 114
Kimsey as CEO, 33, 38
launching and rollout, 30–33
Leonsis and, 34–36
Microsoft takeover attempt, 60–66
as news platform, 39
online advertising, 67
online community, 39–41
P&G marketing concepts, 13
partnerships and, xii–xiii, 56, 62,
  72–75, 86, 132, 138–39
people factor, 139–40
perseverance and, 78
pricing, 65
prominent board members, 104–5
revenue sources, 67
shopping on, 39
stock price, 64, 66, 114, 115
system down crisis (1996), 40–41
Time Warner merger, xi–xiii, 114,
  116–26, 155
as transformational, xii, xiii, xiv
usage surge and problems, 66
valuation, xiii, 114, 116, 123
  "You've got mail" recording, 31–32
AOL Greenhouse, 36–37
Apple, 2, 57, 139, 142, 150, 185, 192
  AOL deal with, 73
  Apple II computers, 42
  App Store, 26

Index

Apple (*cont.*)
  Case, Quantum Computers, and,
    23–29
  executive quote, 189
  iPad, iPhone, or iPod, 3, 70–72, 85
  iTunes and partnerships, 71–72
  MacBook, 85
  Macintosh computer, 25
  self-disruption at, 85
Apple Fellow, 25
Artiphon, 94
AT&T, 56, 115, 116, 130
Atari Inc., 16, 17, 185
Atlantic Records, 136

Bahl, Kunal, 177
Baltimore, Maryland, 95
Barnes & Noble, 132
BellSouth, 17–18
Bell System, 149
benefit or B corporations, 108
Berlin, Germany, 182
Bertolini, Mark, 140
Bewkes, Jeff, 134, 135
Bezos, Jeff, 85
Biden, Joe, 171
Branson, Richard, 122
Brazil, 183
Brin, Sergey, 150, 176
Buffalo, New York, 92
Buffett, Warren, 142
Burch, Tory, 155
Burks, Jewel, 96–97
Bush, George W., 118, 119, 182

cable "open access" fight, 118–19
Canadian Start-Up Visa Program, 181
Cantor, Eric, 158, 159, 160
Carnegie Mellon, 95
Carney, Dan and Frank, 13
Case, Dan, 9–10, 15, 34, 35, 141, 143
Case, Jean, 60, 109, 110, 111
Case, Steve, xii–xiii
  as AOL CEO, 33–34, 38, 39–41,
    56–67, 114–25

AOL launch and rollout, 30–33
AOL Time Warner merger, xi–xiii,
  116–42
AOL Time Warner resignation,
  142
brother Dan and, 9–10, 15, 141
Case Foundation story, 109–11
chair of Jobs Council subcommittee, 156–61
chair of Startup America, 155
co-chair of NACIE, 155
college and side businesses, 10–11
CVC and, 15–22, 186
digital future and, 35
as entrepreneur, 6, 9–11
first business of, Case Enterprises,
  10
first computer course, 11–12
first experience with failure, 17
first startup, 15–20
Gameline and, 17
Hawaiian background of, 93
investment decisions, 92, 93–94
Jobs and the iPod, 71
marriage to Jean Case, 60
message to corporate America,
  192–93
message to entrepreneurs, 189–91
message to the government,
  193–94
message to the reader, 196–99
Microsoft and, 62–66
P&G brand management job,
  12–13
personal statement of, 196–97
Pizza Hut position, 13–14, 185
politics and, 145–46, 155
Quantum Computer Services,
  20–22
Revolution, 54, 74–75, 111, 143–44
Senate testimony, 176
thesis of, on Third Wave, 187–88
Toffler's influence on, 1
uncertainty and career choice,
  185–87

working with the government,
   155–61
Case Foundation, 109–11, 171, 182
Caufield, Frank, 21
CBS, 57
Centers for Disease Control and
   Prevention (CDC), 46, 173
China, xi–xii, 91, 173, 178, 182
Christensen, Clayton M., 85
Cincinnati, Ohio, 98
Cisco Systems, 2
Clinton, Bill, 159–60
Collins, Jim, 139–40
Comcast, 140
Commodore, 19, 22–23, 57, 73
CompuServe, 59–60, 67
Connors, Mike, 40
Consumer Electronics Show, Las
   Vegas (1983), 16–17
Control Video Corporation (CVC),
   15–22, 104, 186
corporate America. *See also* Time
   Warner Inc.
   benefit or B corporations, 108
   Case's message to, 192–93
   conservative mind-set of, 83
   culture of, 140
   disruption and, 80–88, 192
   fostering innovation in, 84, 88, 193
   internal venture funds, 87
   investing in the future, 87–88
   partnerships and, 87, 193
   playing offense and, 87
   predicted failures, 81
   R&D and, 81–82
Coursera, 76
Crain, Jason, 97
Cuba, 183

DARPA, 147
Davis, Donn, 142
Dell, Michael, 155
Dell computers, 155
Detroit, Michigan, 94, 112
Diamandis, Peter, 81

Digital Cities, 36
digital industry and technology, xi,
   xiii, xiv, 12, 17, 35, 39, 45, 91, 109
   digital music, 15–16, 71, 140
   federal government and, 150,
      153–54
   Kodak and, 86
   Time Warner and, 119–20, 122,
      129, 134, 136, 140, 142
Digital Libraries Initiative (DLI), 150
Disney Corporation, 115, 116
disruption, 79, 80–88, 192
   American dominance and, 165–84
   challenge for Fortune 500 CEOs,
      84
   corporate bias toward "no" and, 83
   embracing innovators to manage,
      84
   embracing self-disruption, 85–86
   Kodak and, 86
   playing offense and, 87
   R&D to counter, 81
   Reuters report, 80
   strategy vs., 75
   top companies failing by 2020, 81
   world view of change and, 82–84
Dodd-Frank Wall Street Reform and
   Consumer Protection Act, 157
Doerr, John, 156
dot-com bubble, 3, 127
drones, 76, 77
DuPont, 86
Durham, North Carolina, 91

Earle, Steve, 144
eBay, 3, 115, 116–17
Ebola outbreak (2014), 170–71
Edison, Thomas, 188
education, 5, 47–51, 190
   barriers to entry and, 70
   barriers to innovation in, 50–51
   Kickboard and data for, 99–100
   low-cost teaching experiments,
      49–50
   measuring classroom success, 49

education (*cont.*)
  MOOCs, 75–76
  New Orleans and edtech, 101
  Pear Deck, 47–48
  personalizing the learning process, 48
  Revolution Foods and, 111–13
  Teachers Pay Teachers, 48
  teacher's role and, 49
  technology in the classroom, 47
  venture capital and edtech, 101
  virtual dashboards, 47
Edwards, Elwood, 31–32
Edwards, Karen, 31
Eisenhower, Dwight, 147
Electronic Arts, 115, 116
Electronic Privacy Information Center, 152
Energy Intelligence, 92
entrepreneurs, 6, 7, 9. *See also* Case, Steve; *specific people*
  American dominance and, 7, 165–84
  barriers to entry, 5, 70, 101–2
  Case's message to, 189–91
  Case's message to the reader, 196–99
  corporations vs., 81, 84, 87
  credibility challenge, 72, 76
  cresting of Third Wave and, 55
  crowdfunding and, 157
  disruption and, 79, 80–88
  foreign startup communities, 182
  as future-focused, 83
  geographic concentration of, 90, 91, 188
  geographic diversity and choice of startup locations, 91–98, 188
  government and, 145–64
  healthcare system and, 45
  immigration and, 156, 176–79, 194
  Importance of Startups in Job Creation (chart), 168
  lessons of the First Wave and, 42

  mind-set for, 79
  new job creation and startups, 92–93
  opportunity in New Orleans, 98–101
  in other countries, 181–84
  partnerships, 5, 69–76, 87, 101, 191
  perseverance, 78–79
  Pizza Hut and, 13
  policy issues, 5, 76–78
  "the rise of the rest," 91, 94–105
  rules changing for, 7
  SBA and, 150
  Second Wave and, 3, 5
  social benefit considered by, 107, 188
  Startup America, 110–11
  startup money and, 83, 87, 101
  tax incentives for, 175–76
  Third Wave and, 5, 42–54, 68–79
  three P's for startups, 68–79
  U.S. government and, 78, 146–47, 167–68, 188
  U.S. government and venture capital laws, 156–61, 174–76, 194
  valuation gap in startup location, 103
  Washington, DC as hub, 104–5
Environmental Protection Agency (EPA), 152–53
Ertegun, Ahmet, 136–37
Estrin, James, 86
Etsy, 108
Everyday Health, 74
ExactTarget, 103

Facebook, xiii, 39, 154, 156
  diversity problem, 102
  "move fast and break things," 84
Fadell, Tony, 71
Federal Aviation Administration (FAA), 77
Federal Communications Commission (FCC), 119

FedEx, 84, 155
finance industry, 70, 190
First Wave, xv, 2, 5, 41, 43, 179
    American dominance and, 184
    edtech and, 47
    lessons of, 42
    startup locations, 91
    technology risk of, 77
    Third Wave and, 6, 42
fitness trackers, 45
Fonda, Jane, xi
food, 50–55
    artisan farmers, 54
    barriers to entry and, 70
    bee population and, 52–53
    farm-to-table restaurants, 54–55
    foodtech startups, 54
    millennials and change, 54
    obesity in America and, 112
    Revolution Foods in schools,
        111–13
    safety, 5, 53–54
    size of the industry, 50
    smart packaging, 53
    smart refrigerators, 54
    technology and food production, 52
Food and Drug Administration
    (FDA), 77, 78
Fortune magazine, Global Forum, 140
Freed, Alan, 48
freelance economy, 179–81
Friedman, Milton, 106, 108
Frost, David, 121

GameLine, 16–19, 21
Gates, Bill, 62–64, 65, 142
General Electric (GE), 56, 69, 158
GEnie, 60
    R&D, 84
Germany, 173
Gerstner, Lou, 133–34
Global Center for Digital Business
    Transformation, 80–81
Golden, David, 143

Google, 3, 37, 39, 138–39, 154, 172,
    176, 192
    diversity problem, 102
    search, 150
    self-driving car and, 81
Gore, Al, xiv, 171
GPS navigation, 82, 147, 148
Gretzky, Wayne, 87

H&R Block, 59
Habitat for Humanity, 109
Haig, Al, 104
Hambrecht & Quist (H&Q), 15, 21,
    35, 143
Hastings, Reed, 155
HBO, 119–20, 128, 134
healthcare, 5, 44–46, 190
    barriers to entry and, 70
    biomedical R&D, 173
    Case and Revolution Health, 74
    disease mismanagement, 45–46
    fitness trackers, 45
    health data analysis, 46
    medical and biotech corridor, 90
    misdiagnosis and, 44
    outdated systems and, 44
    startups, 92
    startups, locations of, 95
    tracking epidemics, 46
Helsinki, Finland, 182
Hewlett-Packard (HP), 2
Holden, Christopher, 67
Home Music Store, 15–16, 72
Horowitz, Ben, 115
hotel industry, 192

IBM, 2, 46, 57–58, 69, 73, 92, 133
Idea Village, 101
Immelt, Jeff, 158
immigration, 156, 176–79, 194
    Canadian Start-Up Visa Program, 181
    H-1B visa program, 177–78
    Startup Visa program proposal,
        178

Index

impact investing, 106–13, 188
  Case Foundation story, 109–11
  convergence and, 113
  National Advisory Board, 111
  Revolution Foods, 111–13
  rise of, 107–9
  size of, 113
India, 91, 161, 178
  Snapdeal and, 177
Indiegogo, 157
Innovators, The (Isaacson), xiii
Innovator's Dilemma, The (Christensen), 85
Instacart, 179
Instagram, 4, 39
Intel Corporation, 150
Internet. *See also* First Wave; Second
  Wave; Third Wave
  AOL's importance to, 38–39
  broadband, 118
  cybersecurity and, 151–52
  democratization of, xiv
  early connection costs, 2
  early use, 2–3
  "the eternal September," xiv
  global connectivity, 3
  Gore and, xiv
  government role in, 149–52
  net neutrality rules, 119
  percentage of Americans online
    (1985), xiii
  public access to, xiv
  regulation of, 159–60
  search engines, 3, 150
  service providers, xiv
  social networks, xiii
  worth of economic activity, 149–50
Internet of Everything, 5, 43, 187–88,
  191
Internet of Things, 151–52, 168–69
Isaacson, Walter, xi–xv, 62, 70
Ive, Jonathan, 71

Jarrett, Valerie, 159, 160
Jobs, Steve, 24, 70–72, 85, 142

John Deere, 82
Johnson, Earvin "Magic," 155
Johnson & Johnson, 81
Joswiak, Greg, 70

Kaeser, Joe, 140
Kartsotis, Tom, 94
Kauffman Foundation, 92, 111, 176
Kay, Alan, 25
Kenney, Jason, 181
Kenya, 183
Kesmai, 67
Khan Academy, 49
Kickboard, 99–100
Kickstarter, 94, 108, 157
Kimsey, Jim, 20–21, 27–29, 33, 38, 59
Klain, Ron, 171
Kleiner Perkins Caufield & Byers
  (KPCB), 21, 156
Kobie, Nicole, 52–53
Kodak, 86
Kullman, Ellen, 86

Leonsis, Ted, 34–36, 65, 143
Lerer, Kenny, 124, 125
Levin, Jerry, xii, 120–22, 129–30, 131,
  132, 133, 141
Logan, Don, 134–35
London, 103, 182
  as top city for crowdfunding, 182
Luce, Henry, 117

MacHugh, Will, 53
Malone, John, 64
Mandela, Nelson, 198
Marx, Groucho, 165–66
Massachusetts, 90
McKinsey report on pro-innovation
  policies, 156
Medbery, Jen, 99–100
Microsoft, 2, 56, 60–66
  acquisitions of competitors, 62–64
  AOL acquisition try, 60–66
  MSN and, 63, 64, 65, 66, 67
  Windows 95, 65

millennial generation, 54, 107–8
Mitchell, Kate, 160
mobile apps, 3, 4, 43, 69–70, 95
mobile devices, 3
modems, 2, 17–18, 42, 58, 65
Monsanto, 84
MOOCs (massive open online
    courses), 75–76
Mossberg, Walt, 37
Motley Fool, The, 36
Moviefone, 36
MP3 players, 70
Murdoch, Rupert, 67, 128, 142
Musk, Elon, 68, 176

Napster, 15, 140
NASA, 173
Nashville, Tennessee, 94, 95
National Advisory Council on
    Innovation & Entrepreneurship
    (NACIE), 155
National Institutes of Health, 173
National Science Foundation, 173
Netflix, 155
Netscape, 114–15
New Line Cinema, 128
New Orleans, Louisiana, 90, 98–101
    Hurricane Katrina and, 98–99
    startups in, statistics, 101
News Corp, 67, 128
New York City, 98
New York State, 90
Nigeria, 183
Nixon, Richard M., 170
Nooyi, Indra, 85–86

Obama, Barack, 153, 155–56, 160
    Ebola outbreak (2014) and, 170–71
    "Obama's stealth startup," 153
online gaming, 16–18
online music industry, 70–72

Page, Larry, 150
Park, Todd, 154
Parsons, Dick, 132–35, 141

partnerships, 5
    African proverb and, 69
    AOL and, xii–xiii, 56, 62, 72–75
    Apple and, 23–29, 71–72
    bolstering the internal team, 73–74
    Catch-22 for, 75
    credibility challenge and, 72–76
    Second Wave and, 75
    for the Third Wave, 69–76, 191, 193
Partpic, 96–97
Patagonia, 108
Pathfinder, 122
PayPal, 79
Pear Deck, 47–48
PepsiCo, 85–86
perseverance, 78–79
Pfund, Nancy, 112–13
Picasso, Pablo, 70
Pittman, Bob, 131–32
Pittsburgh, Pennsylvania, 95
Pixar, 142
Pizza Hut, 13–14, 185
PlanetOut, 36–37
Plank, Kevin, 155
policy strategy, 5, 76–78
    regulated industries and, 76–77
POP Biotechnologies, 92
Powell, Colin, 104–5
PowerUP, 109
President's Council on Jobs and
    Competiveness (Jobs Council),
    155–61
Procter & Gamble (P&G), 12–13
Prodigy, 37, 56–57, 58–59, 73

Qualcomm, 150
Quantum Computer Services, 20–26
    AOL launch and rollout, 30–33
    Apple partnership, 23–29
    Commodore and, 22–23
    IBM and, 23, 29
    idea for Internet portal, 28–29, 30
    launching of, 22
    PC-Link, 23, 29
    Q-Link, 23, 29

R&D, 84
  government-funded, 147, 172–74
  Kullman force-out and, 86
  managing disruption and, 81
  100 Award, 147
Raines, Frank, 104
Ravikant, Naval, 160
Reddit, xiii
Redgate Communications, 34–36
Revolution, 54, 111, 143–44, 171
Revolution Foods, 111–13
Revolution Health, 74–75
"Revolution Starts Now, The" (Earle),
  144
Richmond, Kristin Groos, 111–12
"rise of the rest," 94–105, 194
  challenges for, 102–5
  diversity of opportunity and, 101–2
  industry-specific expertise and,
    95–98
  New Orleans, 90, 98–101
  pitch competition, Atlanta, 96
  startup location diversity, 91–98,
    188
  valuation gap in startup location,
    103
  venture capital and, 93–98, 103
Roberts, Brian, 140
robotics technology, 95
Roosevelt, Theodore, 53
  "man in the arena" speech, 198–99
Ross, Steve, 117
Rotenberg, Marc, 152

Salesforce, 103
Samuelsohn, Darren, 168–69
Sandberg, Sheryl, 156
San Francisco, California, 98
Sarbanes-Oxley legislation, 157
Sasson, Steven, 86
Savage, Tige, 143
Schiller, Phil, 71
Sears, 57
Second Wave, xv, 3–4, 42, 87, 179
  American dominance and, 184

apps and success in, 69–70
characteristics of, 43
dorm-inspired apps, 5
edtech and, 47
location of entrepreneurs and, 91,
  95
market risk of, 77
partnerships not needed, 75
peaking of, 43
success stories, 96
technology focus of, 95
Securities and Exchange Commission
  (SEC), 77, 175
self-driving car, 76, 81–82, 190
Seriff, Marc, 15–16, 20, 21, 27, 29, 33
Shackleton, Ernest, 186
Shazam, 97
Shinola, 94
Shockley, William, 104
Siemens, 84, 140
Silicon Valley, 6, 15, 43, 90, 95, 105,
  114–15, 186, 188
  culture of innovation, 43
  Cupertino, Case, and Apple, 23–26
  diversity problem, 102
  foreign-born company founders,
    176
  government and, 150–51
  relationship with the federal gov-
    ernment, 163–64, 194–95
  start of tech in, 104
Skype, 116, 136
Small Business Administration
  (SBA), 150
Smalltalk programming language, 25
smartphones, 3, 43, 45
Smith, Clive, 19–20
Smith, Fred, 155
Smith, Megan, 37
Smithsonian's American History Mu-
  seum, Places of Invention, 105
Snapchat, xiii, 41, 43
Snapdeal, 177
Social Impact Investment Taskforce,
  108

social networks, xiii, 3, 43
Solow, Robert, 174
Source, The, 15
South by Southwest (SXSW) conference (2014), 111, 112
South Korea, 173, 182, 183
Soylent, 51
Special Olympics, 109
Sperling, Gene, 159
Spotify, 15, 39
Sprint, 2, 67
Startup America, 110–11, 155
Start-Up Chile, 181–82, 183
startups. *See* entrepreneurs
Stockholm, 182
Sun Microsystems, 2
SUNY at Buffalo, 92
Surowiecki, James, 178
Sweetgreen, 54

Tandy, 73
TCI (Tele-Communications Inc.), 64
Teachers Pay Teachers, 48
Teach for America, 99, 101
telecommunications, 15, 149, 196
Tesla, 176
Thalberg, Irving, 165
Thiel, Peter, 163
Third Wave, xv, 4–5, 42–55, 68–79
    adaptability and, 78–79
    American dominance and, 165–84
    assets for, 87
    barriers to entry and, 5, 42, 70
    Case's thesis, 187–88
    companies, new regional areas, 91–94
    cresting of, 55
    disruption and, 75, 79, 80–88
    education and, 47–51, 70
    finance industry and, 70
    First Wave and, 6, 42
    food and, 51–55, 70
    future scenario, 89–90
    government and, 146–47, 151–72, 188

healthcare and, 5, 44–46, 70
    impact investing, 106–13
    infrastructure for, 42
    Internet of Everything, 5, 43, 187–88
    mantra for, 47
    millennial generation and, 54, 107–8
    partnerships and, 69–76, 87, 191, 193
    perseverance and, 78–79
    policy issues and, 5, 76–78
    policy risk, 78
    regulated industries of, 76–77, 191
    "the rise of the rest" and, 94–105
    single greatest startup challenge, 72
    startups superstars for, 68–69
    success stories, 96
    as tech-enabled not tech-centric, 95
    transformative economic value, 101–2, 113
    transportation and, 70
    who will win in, 79
Third Wave, The (Toffler), 1, 7, 12
Time Inc., 62, 117, 128, 134
Time magazine, 117, 129
    "news tour" to China (199), xi
    partnership with AOL for online content, xii–xiii
Time Warner
    acquisitions, 117–18
    AOL merger, xii–xiii, 114, 116–42, 155
    board of directors, 135–36, 140–41
    content brands, 118, 119–20
    dot-com bubble and, 127
    formation of, 117
    Internet and, 62, 121–22, 134–35
    operations of, 128, 134–35
    revenues and profits, 118
Time Warner Cable, 120, 128, 130, 134, 136
Time Warner Ventures, 143
Tobey, Kirsten Saenz, 111–12

Index

Toffler, Alvin, 1, 7, 12, 14
Towers Watson, 74
transportation, 190
  barriers to entry and, 70
  self-driving car, 76, 81–82, 190
  supersonic Hyperloop, 190
  Third Wave and, 5
  Uber, 81, 83–84, 161–63, 179
  U.S. Department of Transportation
    as Third Wave customer and,
    153
Turner, Ted, xi, 118, 122, 129
Turner Broadcasting System (TBS),
  118, 119–20, 128, 129
23andMe, 78
Twitter, xiii, 4, 39, 43, 154

Uber, 81, 83–84, 161–63, 179
Under Armour, 155
United Kingdom, 182
UPS, 84
U.S. Department of Defense (DOD),
  Third Wave integration and, 153
U.S. Department of Transportation
  (DOT), 153
US Digital Service (USDS), 153–54
U.S. government, 145–64
  agencies and the digital age,
    153–54
  American dominance and, 165–84
  Case and how to work with the
    government, 155–61
  Case's message to, 193–94
  as customer, 152–54
  cybersecurity and, 151–52
  DARPA, 147
  data, regulation of, 151
  Digital Libraries Initiative (DLI),
    150
  entrepreneurial environment and,
    146–47, 167–68, 188
  getting in front of the Third Wave,
    168–72
  immigration laws, 156, 176–79, 194

  as innovator, 147–51
  Internet and, xiv, 149–50
  Internet regulations, 159–60
  JOBS Act, 159–60, 174–75
  new rules for a new era and,
    179–81
  R&D investing by, 147, 172–74
  reforming Senate confirmation and
    vetting process, 170–71
  regulated industries, 76–77, 191
  regulatory function, 151
  Silicon Valley and, 163–64, 194–95
  size of the cabinet and, 170
  startups vs. small businesses and,
    167–68
  Telecommunications Act (1996),
    149
  Third Wave czar proposed, 172
  Uber and, 161–63
  venture capital laws, 156–61,
    174–76, 194

venture capital, 83. *See also* impact
    investing
  Case's decisions in, 92, 93–94
  Case's largest check, 94
  corporate funding of entrepre-
    neurs, 87
  edtech and, 101
  federal regulations and, 156–61,
    174–76, 194
  focus on return, 106
  geographic concentration of, 90
  geographic diversity of, 93–98
  internal venture funds, 87
  rise-of-the-rest pitch competition,
    96–97
  seeking biggest idea, 83
  valuation gap in startup location,
    103
  West Bank and, 182
video games, 16–17
Virgin Group, 122
von Meister, Bill, 15–16, 72, 104, 186

Wall Street Journal (WSJ)
  AOL review by Mossberg, 37–38
  AOL's IPO and, 34
  AOL Time Warner merger story,
    128
Warby Parker, 108
Warner, Mark, 180
Warner Brothers, 118, 119, 128
Warner Communications, 16, 117
Warner Music, 16, 118, 128, 136
Washington, DC, 104–5, 144
Washington Post
  negative stories on AOL, 137
  "Unconventional Transactions
    Boosted Sales," 137
Waze, 4
Wharton School, report on impact
    funds, 109
WhatsApp, 116

"What Washington Really Knows
    About the Internet of Things"
    (Samuelsohn), 168–69
Wheeler, Tom, 119
Whitman, Meg, 117
Wiggins, Betti, 112
Williams, Tennessee, 98
Williams College, 10–12, 145
Williamson, Tim, 101

Xerox PARC, 25
XPRIZE, 81

YouTube, 39

Zakaria, Fareed, 91
Zappos, 103
Zients, Jeff, 159, 160
Zuckerberg, Mark, 3, 84